Day Camp Programming and Administration

Core Skills and Practices

Jill Moffitt

Human Kinetics

Library of Congress Cataloging-in-Publication Data

Moffitt, Jill.
  Day camp programming and administration : core skills and practices / Jill
Moffitt.
      p. cm.
  Includes bibliographical references and index.
  ISBN-13: 978-0-7360-7517-6 (soft cover)
  ISBN-10: 0-7360-7517-8 (soft cover)
  1. Day camps. 2. Day camps--Management. 3. Recreation leadership. I. Title.
  GV197.D3M64 2011
  796.54'23--dc22

                                                            2011009465

ISBN-10: 0-7360-7517-8 (print)
ISBN-13: 978-0-7360-7517-6 (print)

The web addresses cited in this text were current as of May 2011, unless otherwise noted.

Acquisitions Editor: Gayle Kassing, PhD; **Developmental Editor:** Ray Vallese; **Assistant Editor:** Derek Campbell; **Special Projects Editor:** Anne Cole; **Copyeditor:** Patsy Fortney; **Indexer:** Bobbi Swanson; **Permission Manager:** Dalene Reeder; **Graphic Designer:** Nancy Rasmus; **Graphic Artists:** Denise Lowry and Angela K. Snyder; **Cover Designer:** Keith Blomberg; **CD Face Designer:** Susan Rothermel Allen; **Photographer (cover):** ©Eyewire (main photo) and ©Human Kinetics (insets); **Photographer (interior):** ©Human Kinetics, unless otherwise specified; photo on p. 4 ©Eyewire; photos on pp. 9, 27, 140, and 171 courtesy of Jill Moffitt; photos on pp. 11 and 69 ©Terry Wild Stock Inc.; photo on p. 20 ©Eric Isselée; photos on pp. 21 and 38 ©Jim West; photo on p. 34 ©AP Photo/Harry Cabluck; photo on p. 45 ©Human Kinetics/Les Woodrum; photo on p. 85 ©Phototake/David M. Grossman; photo on p. 96 ©Edie Layland; photo on p. 111 ©Phototake/Abraham Menashe; photo on p. 123 ©AP Photo/Kalamazoo Gazette, Tanner Curtis; photo on p. 132 ©John Birdsong/PA Photos; photo on p. 137 ©Image100; photo on p. 147 ©AP Photo/Phil Coale; photo on p. 149 ©Bold Stock/age fotostock; and photo on p. 152 ©Digitalpress/fotolia.com; **Photo Asset Manager:** Laura Fitch; **Visual Production Assistant:** Joyce Brumfield; **Photo Production Manager:** Jason Allen; **Art Manager:** Kelly Hendren; **Associate Art Manager:** Alan L. Wilborn; **Illustrator:** ©Human Kinetics; **Printer:** United Graphics

Printed in the United States of America   10   9   8   7   6   5   4   3   2   1

The paper in this book is certified under a sustainable forestry program.

Human Kinetics
Web site: www.HumanKinetics.com

United States: Human Kinetics, P.O. Box 5076, Champaign, IL 61825-5076
800-747-4457
e-mail: humank@hkusa.com

Canada: Human Kinetics, 475 Devonshire Road Unit 100, Windsor, ON N8Y 2L5
800-465-7301 (in Canada only)
e-mail: info@hkcanada.com

Europe: Human Kinetics, 107 Bradford Road, Stanningley, Leeds LS28 6AT, United Kingdom
+44 (0) 113 255 5665
e-mail: hk@hkeurope.com

Australia: Human Kinetics, 57A Price Avenue, Lower Mitcham, South Australia 5062
08 8372 0999
e-mail: info@hkaustralia.com

New Zealand: Human Kinetics, P.O. Box 80, Torrens Park, South Australia 5062
0800 222 062
e-mail: info@hknewzealand.com

E4518

CONTENTS

Contents

Recreational day camps are an important part of many people's childhoods. Municipality-run and privately owned camps have been serving children through innovative camp programs for over 100 years. College and university recreation departments in the United States have also created summer programs to serve community members as well as to secure supplemental funding to operate their departments throughout the fiscal year. As day camps continue to prove financially lucrative, more and more campus recreation professionals have become interested in starting similar programs for their communities. These professionals want to know how to plan, organize, implement, and evaluate a summer camp program at their colleges and universities.

I have worked in the camping world since 1998. Year after year, aspiring camp administrators have asked me how to design summer camp programs. Although I have been happy to oblige with recommendations, referrals, and mini-consultations, I began to recognize the need for an administrative camp manual. After researching the resources currently available, I discovered that of the handful of books specific to camp management, none were specific to facility-based camps. Furthermore, despite a plethora of programmatic resources available to camp administrators, many required equipment and large financial resources that I believe are not realistic for the common facility-based camp. Having served in a variety of capacities in campus recreation, municipality-run, and privately owned camps during my career, I have noted that these various facilities face common problems. Thus, I saw the need for a comprehensive resource that provides basic information, examples, suggestions, and considerations for the facility-based camp administrator.

Day Camp Programming and Administration: Core Skills and Practices was developed to serve facility-based camp administrators working in municipalities, college campuses, and privately owned fitness facilities.

The facilities at college campuses, municipal recreation departments, and private fitness organizations are generally designed to serve adults. For this reason, the first question these organizations must ask when looking to design day camps is *How do we design programs for children in facilities that are not as child-friendly as we would like a day camp facility to be?* This book will help professionals working in municipal recreation departments, fitness center owners and operators, and campus recreation professionals consider their options in outfitting their facilities to serve children.

All of these types of organizations are also concerned with managing risk and following safety regulations to protect their patrons. The addition of young campers and camp staff may require that organizations institute additional safeguards such as requiring that parents and guardians sign release of liability waivers and permission slips for field trips, setting strict rules regarding camper drop-off and pickup, following safety standards for equipment and health standards for distributing food and medicine to campers, using age-appropriate games safely, and training a qualified staff to ensure that campers are physically and emotionally safe at camp.

Finally, organizations must consider the financial implications of a day camp and aim to generate revenue that will increase the fiscal sustainability of the organization as a whole. In addition to providing high-quality programming that serves a community need, day camps can become lucrative endeavors when they are planned, organized, and implemented well. This book explains how to develop a camp program that is fiscally sound and provides a healthy return on the initial investment. Although organizations differ in their objectives, goals, and outcomes, they are similar in their desire to offer successful day camps.

All of these issues and more are discussed in this book. In addition, the CD-ROM includes numerous forms and examples, including registration materials, waivers, medical documents, emergency action plans, checklists, logs, evaluations, and more. The ready-to-use forms can be printed and put to work in camps as is, and the examples provide administrators with models to follow when creating their own camp-specific forms. For technical details about accessing the materials on the CD-ROM, see the last page of the book.

Day Camp Programming and Administration: Core Skills and Practices begins with a general overview and background information on the camping world. Chapter 1 offers a brief history of organized camping, outlines the benefits of camp for children, and describes the various types of camps. Program-based and facility-based camps are highlighted, followed by sport camps, recreational camps, and educational camps, to name a few. The core skills and practices begin with chapter 2, which addresses the basic considerations of conducting community surveys, including instrument selection, participant selection, survey distribution, data interpretation, camp inventory needs, market analysis, program decisions, fiscal accountability, and strategic planning strategies and suggestions.

The book then moves into the practical requirements for successful camp programs. Chapter 3 identifies several areas that address the integrity of the camp, such as laws and legislation, health and safety standards, and programming safety. Chapter 4 addresses policy development and enforcement. Policies regarding registration, refunds, drop-off and pickup, discipline, and parental communication are outlined in addition to everyday policies concerning issues such as inclement weather, illness, attire, sunscreen, and distributing medicine at camp.

Chapter 5 addresses the administrative functions necessary for camps to operate smoothly, such as the registration process, the financial blueprint, the organizational structure of the day camp, and the daily program schedule. Chapters 6 and 7 describe methods for hiring personnel and selecting activities for the program. These chapters address staff qualifications, hiring procedures, staff training, ongoing staff development, performance evaluations, counselor-in-training programs, program descriptions, and program selection and implementation. The book concludes with chapter 8, which covers soliciting feedback from staff, parents, and campers regarding the overall camp program. It prescribes methods for distributing and analyzing both qualitative and quantitative evaluation tools that help camp administrators make decisions about future camp offerings.

Creating a summer camp program or renovating a current program is exciting and rewarding. With proper planning, implementation, and evaluation strategies, you can develop programs that become staples of your community for years to come. A healthy camp program is always changing, growing, and being reshaped to fit the changing needs of the community and achieve the organizational mission. Camp programs enrich children's lives, build strong families, and create supportive communities. A solid summer camp program is an investment that can reap large returns when it is done safely, appropriately, and efficiently.

Hopefully, the information, strategies, forms, and suggestions in *Day Camp Programming and Administration: Core Skills and Practices* will be useful in your facility-based camp and provide some practical solutions for innovative program design, budgeting, safety and risk management, strategic planning, staffing and training, and evaluation. The information in this book and CD-ROM is not all-inclusive but it is easy to understand, easy to apply, and easy to evaluate. Happy camping!

ACKNOWLEDGMENTS

Thanks to my family, friends, and coworkers who helped me with this book throughout every stage of the process. I would like to acknowledge Barbara Brimi, Jeff Moffitt, and Ashlie Rice for motivating me and keeping me going at different points in the writing process. I extend major thanks to my colleagues in the field, Gregg Bates, Jason Adamowicz, and Tara Yesenski, who provided a lot of material and saved me a lot of work. A special thanks to my coworkers at the University of North Carolina, Bill Haggard, Dominique Ennis, Jeremy Engel, Nolan LaVoie, Leah McDowell, Debby Schwartz, and Rosie Palmisano, who covered for me during weeks of writing away from the office. Finally, thanks to Gayle Kassing, Ray Vallese, and all of the editors at Human Kinetics. If patience is a virtue, then they are the most virtuous group of people I have ever met.

Reviewing Organized Camping

The term *camping* often calls to mind pitching a tent, staying overnight in a park or forest, and fishing for food while reconnecting with nature. Organized camping is specifically for children, but the concept is the same. Indeed, organized camping today is based on the traditional idea of going into a wooded area and connecting with nature, and because it is specific to children, food, shelter, security, and basic needs are provided. At least this is how organized camping began over 140 years ago. Today, with an ever-changing world and ever-changing ideas about adolescence, families, and citizenship development, the world of organized camping has had to branch out and provide a variety of services to meet the needs of people in various geographic locations.

Many camp programs are offered through town parks and recreation departments. Some communities have access to local camps where children can participate in overnight or day camp fun. As populations have grown, community recreation departments have been faced with the challenge of providing day camps in facilities that were not constructed with organized camping in mind. Yet, time and again, municipalities and recreation centers have met this challenge by creatively scheduling shared facilities, modifying activities to make use of limited resources or equipment, and providing these services at a reasonable cost.

Colleges and universities are no different from municipalities and town recreation departments. With different types of students attending, larger continuing education populations, and a commitment to reach out to the larger community, it is fitting that campus recreation departments have also answered the call of service.

The challenges campus and community recreation organizations face in designing, planning, developing, staffing, and maintaining children's recreational day camps are many, but manageable. Recreational camps provided in facilities not intended to serve the needs of organized camping are known as facility-based camps (Lantz, 1955). Unlike organized camps housed in facilities on private or public grounds that were built specifically as day camps for children, facility-based camps must adjust to the capabilities of the facilities they are using and the resources surrounding them. Older, antiquated organized camps with no money to update their facilities may also find themselves in similar situations.

Why did this call to service arise in local private, public, and nonprofit recreation organizations? How did the world of organized camping find itself knocking on communities' doors? To understand why community camp services are provided today, we look at the history of organized camping, highlight its benefits for children, and discuss the basic types of camps as derived from the literature.

Brief History of Organized Camping

The Gunnery Camp is on record as the first organized camping program in the United States (American Camp Association [ACA], 2010a). It was founded in 1861 by Fredrick W. Gunn and his wife Abigail in Washington, Connecticut. The Gunns ran a boys' home school and decided to take the boys on a two-week trip. On this trip they set up camp and spent their time boating, fishing, and trapping. The trip was a huge success, and the Gunns continued the tradition for 12 years. A year after the Gunns ended their traditional camping trips, the first YWCA camp opened in Philadelphia.

The Vacation Project was the YWCA's first camp at Asbury Park, New Jersey; it consisted of a summer boarding and vacation house for "tired young women wearing out their lives in an almost endless drudgery for wages that admit no thought of rest or recreation" (ACA, 2010a). In 1876, the first private camp was founded by Dr. Joseph Trimble Roth near Wilkes-Barre, Pennsylvania. The idea behind the North Mountain School of Physical Culture was to take "weakly boys out into camp life in the woods, so that the pursuit of health could be combined with the practical knowledge outside usual academic lines" (ACA, 2010a). In 1885, the YMCA caught up with the YWCA by offering a camping trip for seven boys in Newburgh, New York, which in six years expanded to 83 campers. And by 1900, the first Boys' Club camp was founded in Salem, Massachusetts, to entertain 76 boys over the course of seven weeks during the summer (ACA, 2010a).

In 1910, the American Camp Association (ACA) was founded under its original name, the Camp Directors Association of America (CDAA), by Alan S. Williams, who created a model for standardizing the organized camping experience. Also, in 1910, the Boy Scouts of America founded the first BSA camp at Lake George, New York. Soon after, Dr. Luther Halsey Gulick founded the Camp Fire Girls, which today is known as Camp Fire. The CDAA merged with the National Association of Directors of Girls' Camps in 1924 and changed its name to the Camp Director Association, until 1935, when it changed its name again to the American Camp Association. Today, the ACA is located in Martinsville, Indiana, and boasts a membership of over 7,000 professionals (ACA, 2010a).

From 1930 to 1948, organized camping was conducted in much the same way as the original programs, serving various groups and taking place around the country. With the help of the National Park Service, many camps without campgrounds were able to rent camping space in the Recreational Demonstration Areas that were created across the country during the 1930s.

In 1948, however, the ACA adopted Williams' standards for camping programs, which became the basis for ACA accreditation and changed the way camping was offered. The ACA standards were nationally recognized in a court of law and required providers to serve in good faith to meet these standards. Today, there are 300 standards for health safety and programming in camps. However, despite the ACA's adoption of standards in the late 1940s, in the late 1990s, government agencies and organizations began to wonder whether the camp experience was beneficial enough to justify investments in organized camping (ACA, 2010c).

Despite a number of studies conducted during the early and mid-1900s, there simply was not enough money to conduct research that could make a legitimate argument for beneficial outcomes on a larger scale. As a result, although camping professionals were very sure of the positive experience camps afforded children, they were unable to solidify government and financial support outside of the ACA. Eventually, the Lilly Endowment, an Indiana-based foundation that supports efforts that advance education, religion, and community development, bestowed a grant on the ACA and charged it with identifying benefits and outcomes using scientific rigor.

In *Organized Camping: A Historical Perspective,* Ramsing (2007) describes the four phases in the development of organized camping: (1) the recreation phase (1861 to 1920), (2) the education phase (1920 to 1950), (3) the social orientation and reasonability phase (1940 to 1970), and (4) the new directions phase (1970 to the present). These phases describe camp programmers' focus during those times in their efforts to provide experiential education opportunities that help develop boys and girls into actively engaged adult citizens.

Evidence-Based Benefits of Organized Camping

Until recently, there was little evidence-based research on the benefits of organized camping, which limited camp professionals' ability to establish programs that required a large amount of support. However, in the last 12 years, the research on camp benefits to children has grown exponentially (Diana, 2001), revealing how camps help children become engaged citizens. The following sections outline the current literature that reveals that organized camping benefits society as well as the children it serves.

Supporting Research

A handful of studies have examined the benefits of recreational camps in terms of psychological development, social growth, and self-esteem, but the studies do not offer program administrators guidelines for developing these positive outcomes (ACA, 2010b; Dottavio, O'Leary, & Koth, 1980; Draper, 1975; Duncan, 1956; Harter, 1990). Rather, the studies have concentrated on selling camps to local communities to gain both financial and political support. Shivers (1989) highlighted psychological benefits of camp and described logistical considerations found in summer camp settings as a way to suggest how to schedule camps but

Organized camping offers many benefits for children, including improved psychological development, social growth, and self-esteem.

offered no specific guidelines regarding camp activities. Additionally, qualitative research on organized camping has focused on the characteristics of camps in certain parts of the United States (Smith, 1991), making generalizing the finding to a larger population difficult (Hultsmann, 1999).

Research has shown that programs that are supported by the public and cater to the needs of participants exhibit longevity and financial stability (Marsh, 1999). The importance of financial accountability when evaluating camp operations should not be underestimated (Rothschild, 2001). The need to keep programs and schedules in mind before making drastic changes to budgets can help ensure the efficient use of time, money, and energy. Camps that do not adapt to the changing needs of their constituents risk financial suicide (Rothschild, 2001).

Additional studies have looked at the operations, program trends, and patron satisfaction of camps for children with disabilities (Lee, 1972; Marsh, 1999; Sullivan & O'Brien, 2001). Lee, an advocate for differently able populations and a researcher, examined the role of high-quality outdoor recreation programs on the self-constructs of disabled campers and reported a positive correlation (1972). Marsh, a leading researcher in organized camping, examined several benefits of camping for children with disabilities and found a positive correlation between camp programs and self-esteem (1999). Sullivan, a graduate student at Indiana University, edited a three-year research project to determine the current practices of camps providing inclusive activities for children with disabilities (2001). The findings of these studies are helpful to camps catering to the needs of children

CAMP COUNSEL

Organized Camping Today

The evolution of organized camping in the United States has been an exciting journey where child development, programming, and recreational pursuits are concerned. Since the first outdoor camping excursion at The Gunnery Camp, professionals interested in the field have understood the value of organized camping for building the self-esteem of American youth. Today, organized camping in the United States has become a staple of child development and engaged citizenship. Below is a list of facts about organized camping that demonstrates its impact on American culture, society, and youth development.

- Eleven million children and adults attend camp annually (ACA, 2010c).
  - A total of $150,000 is given annually in scholarships to over 100 children.
  - Ninety percent of ACA-accredited camps offer some form of financial assistance to over 1 million children who are from economically deprived families, have special medical needs, or have special situations that might preclude them from attending camp.
- There are 12,000 organized camps in the United States, and 2,545 are accredited by the American Camp Association (2010c).
  - 7,000 residential camps
  - 5,000 day camps (an increase of nearly 90 percent in the past 20 years)
  - 6,200 operated in the nonprofit sector
  - 2,300 operated in the private sector
- Eight reasons for camping (Northern Arizona University, 2001):
  - Reconnect with the outdoor world.
  - Get away from the daily grind and everyday routine.
  - Connect with one's cultural heritage.
  - Take time to "rough it."
  - Develop qualities in the physical, mental, social, spiritual learning domains.
  - Develop skills and positive attitudes.
  - Maintain social connections with family and friends.
  - Take time for personal involvement, personal enrichment, and personal renewal.

Adapted, by permission, from Northern Arizona University. Available: http://www.prm.nau.edu/prm280/chap1_lesson.htm; American Camp Association. Available: http://www.acacamps.org/media-center/camp-trends/fact

with disabilities but do little to guide administrators of facility-based camps for able-bodied populations.

Other studies have examined the role of recreational programs in the physical activity and lifestyle choices made as adults (Pate et al., 1996; Taylor et al., 1999; Trudeau et al., 1999). These studies advance the argument that recreation programs offer healthy outlets for youth during the summer months when they may be the most inactive (Willits & Willits, 1986). Success in physical activities outside of physical education courses can encourage continued participation in physical activity (Pate et al., 1996).

The literature also includes research that highlights adolescent and preteen physical activity and sport participation patterns across race, gender, and class. This research outlines general considerations for programming, although they are not specific to facility-based camps. Many studies have focused on understanding the attitudes and opinions of teenagers in grades 9 through 12 and revealed differences in participation and perceptions based on race and gender (Grimmer & Williams, 2001; Henderson, 1996; Lefstein et al., 1982; Mourão-Carvalhal, Vasconcelos-Raposo, & Malina, 2001; Pawelko & Magafus, 1997; Pellegrini, 1992; Phillip, 1998; Ruiz, 2000; Smith, 1991).

Phillip compared black and white adolescents' (ages 11 to 13) perceptions of recreation services and playtime, noting a difference between the races concerning gender participation. White adolescents recognized a fundamental difference between men and women in terms of physical activity choices, whereas black adolescents did not. White adolescents consented that males tended to pick more physically aggressive activities most often found in traditional sports dominated by men, such as basketball and football, whereas females tended to pick less aggressive activities such as softball, volleyball, and track. This recognition was not mirrored in black adolescents, who consented that both males and females chose a range of activities regardless of aggression levels (Grimmer & Williams, 2001; Henderson, 1996; Lefstein et al., 1982; Mourão-Carvalhal, Vasconcelos-Raposo, & Malina, 2001; Pawelko & Magafus, 1997; Pellegrini, 1992; Phillip, 1998; Ruiz, 2000; Smith, 1991).

Research based in Canada has provided a framework for developing recreational programs for youth and children and indicated the ramifications of recreation on Canadian at-risk youth (Canadian Parks and Recreation Association, 1998; Ontario [Canada] Ministry of Citizenship, Culture and Recreation; SMC Management Services, Inc.; and Grassroots Enterprises, 1998). The authors detail current statistics related to healthy child development and provide many points of consideration when creating programs for adolescents. One consistent suggestion was that programmers listen to youths regarding their needs and desires.

Professionals providing programs for adolescents should be especially attuned to the needs of preteens because many young people cease participation in recreational activities after the age of 13 (Phillip, 1998). Quality programs beginning at the preteen level can encourage future participation (Phillip, 1998). The decrease in participation at 13 has been attributed to lack of money, a sport focus, an adult program focus, class and racial discrimination, a lack of transportation, disinterest in the recreation program structure and offerings, a lack of adequate information describing offerings, and a lack of family and parental support (Ontario [Canada] Ministry of Citizenship et al., 1998). Strategies have been offered for increasing recreation participation within this population in Canada (Edwards, 2000), but few have looked at encouraging participation choices through recreational day camps in the United States.

The shortage of research on recreational day camp programming for preteens hampers administrators' efforts to serve this heterogeneous population in a structured environment. Moreover, little is known about what preteens consider desirable recreational day camp programming. Camps targeting adolescent populations by offering a variety of programs may be successful; however, no data have been published identifying reasons for program popularity from the middle school perspective.

Developmental Benefits to Children

What does all of this research mean for you? In summation, strong evidence supports the notion that camps benefit children by helping them develop leadership and communication skills and increasing their participation, responsibility, resourcefulness, resilience, caring, fairness, citizenship, and trustworthiness (ACA, 2010c). Additional research provides a solid foundation of evidence of the cognitive benefits of organized camping in relation to academic achievement (West & Crompton, 2001). A larger body of knowledge supports the suggestion that participation in camps also decreases undesirable behavior and poor choices among youth, particularly youth classified as at-risk. Scholars report that children engaged in camp programs are less likely to drop out of school, become pregnant as teens, make poor decisions that lead to deviant behavior, and experience feelings of powerlessness (Marsh, 1999; Widmer, Ellis, & Trunnell, 1996).

The literature also addresses the affective domain of learning, providing anecdotes that suggest that participation in organized camp programs helps children develop healthy coping skills for dealing with the injustices of life (Marsh, 1999; Ravenscroft & Markwell, 2000; Warder, 1973). Finally, the most resounding evidence in the field indicates that organized camping participation encourages healthy living through fun, engaging, and challenging activities that promote lifelong learning (Fletcher, 1973; Hartmann, 2001; Marsh, 1999; Rule, 1998).

It is important to note that most studies focused on children aged 10 to 18. Studies that focused on children aged 5 to 9 were significantly more anecdotal, resulting in inconclusive data (Diana, 2001; Sibthorp, 2000; Taylor, 2001; Walton, 2001). However, in almost every study specific to this age range that was reviewed, the common benefits were in the social and emotional domains of learning. Evidence extracted from these studies suggests that campers 5 to 9 years old learn appropriate social roles, develop skills in leisure-time and recreational activities, engage in self-discovery, and begin to learn to channel emotional energies into constructive activities.

These findings are consistent with the data from general leisure studies as a whole and can be further examined in the context of Jensen's hierarchy of leisure (1977). The hierarchy of leisure suggests that the less engaged a person is in leisure-time activities, the less engaged the person will be in personal and engaged citizenship, classified as "service to others" (Henderson et al., 2001). The hierarchy of leisure was not intended to apply to youth, but given the benefits and outcomes of organized camping identified in the literature, it is tempting to assume that a correlation exists, although further study is necessary.

At any rate, the literature suggests that camps may have a much greater role in personal development throughout the life span than what has currently been identified. To what extent, at this juncture in the evolution of scholarly discovery, is unclear. What is clear is that organized camping has an important role in the development of children socially, cognitively, physically, and emotionally across age groups (Thurber et al., 2007). You can use this knowledge in planning day camps, regardless of the recreational sector you work in (public, private, or nonprofit) or whether you are starting or revitalizing a program. Outcome-based research can help you secure additional funding for camp programs, sell changes or initiatives to communities, and identify areas in which to specialize based on resources, funding, and community demographics.

To create a successful camp program, you need to determine the outcomes and benefits you believe will be achievable within the context of your camp. The first step in this dance is to determine the type of camp best suited to your organization and the kinds of programming available. Later chapters of this book offer suggestions and resources for programming considerations for a variety of recreational sectors. For now, we offer a brief outline of the types of camps that exist within the scope of organized camping.

Types of Camps

Before examining the types of camps, we need to distinguish among the sectors that exist within the larger recreation and leisure field. Three recreational sectors are referred to throughout this book: private, public/government, and nonprofit. All three are important in servicing the needs of communities, and each requires unique strategies to succeed. Depending on the scope of funding, resources, and clientele, camps can be public, private, nonprofit, or any combination of the three. Facility-based commonalities across these three sectors are highlighted as a means for providing a general overview of program-based camps versus facility-based camps. Additionally, it's important to remember that a variety of specialty areas (performance art camps, sport camps, computer camps, math camps, and so on) exist within the classifications of program-based camps and facility-based camps.

Program-Based Camps

Traditional, program-based camps use facilities that were built to suit the needs of the camp. They often include a dining hall, several bathroom facilities, cabins, large open fields for activities and games, an arts and crafts cabin, a nature cabin, outdoor sport courts, a barn and stable for horseback riding, wooded areas with identified overnight campsites, ropes courses and climbing walls, outdoor swimming areas such as lakes with docks for waterfront activities, and a main camp office.

Program-based camps are ideal settings for camp administrators. Questions of what types of programs the facilities will be able to accommodate safely are often resolved during the facility design phase. Large open fields allow for activities such as archery, soccer, baseball, capture the flag, mat-ball, kickball, New Games, innovative games, and a host of other games and activities that appeal to children and are developmentally appropriate across varying stages of development.

Facility-Based Camps

Facility-based camps generally use facilities that have existed long before day camp programming was considered. In contrast to program-based camps, facility-based camps require ingenuity and compromise to develop programming that is

Program-based camps often have large open fields, which provide the setting for many different kinds of games and activities.

current, fun, and innovative in facilities that may be outdated or ill suited, or that were constructed for adult recreationalists rather than child campers. An obvious solution may be to simply upgrade or construct new facilities. However, renovating and building facilities can be expensive, and few organizations have the money or community support to do so. This is especially true for public and nonprofit organizations whose funding is either provided by tax dollars or set by the cost of tuition.

Private organizations may have a better chance of raising funds for upgraded and new facilities. However, many of these organizations are governed by boards of directors or trustees who may not want to spend money on this type of endeavor or hesitate passing the cost on to club members.

Funding is just one factor that distinguishes the three sectors (public, private, and nonprofit); others are highlighted throughout this section. To understand the division of these sectors more fully, it's important to note that in most cases (but certainly not all) facility-based camps are offered through municipal parks and recreation departments, college campuses, and private fitness clubs; these will be briefly outlined in the following sections.

Municipality Camps

Municipalities offering day camps often depend on access to school facilities during the summer months. Very small town recreation departments may not have their own recreation centers in which to hold day camps, and larger city parks and recreation departments may not have enough recreation centers to serve the needs of the entire population. Regardless, the varying issues municipalities face in providing day camps cause administrators to depend a great deal on facilities such as school buildings, which are accessible, inexpensive, familiar to the community, and conveniently located.

For some day camp activities, school facilities may be ideal. For example, a school art room would be ideal for an arts and crafts program. However, designing, implementing, and maintaining programs in facilities ill suited for organized camping require innovation and creativity as well as adaptability and flexibility. This is especially true when community buildings such as schools are shared during the summer months with other users. To maintain quality camp programming, you must be willing to be flexible in working with other facility users.

Campus Recreation Camps

Day camps on college campuses are typically managed by or housed in the recreation or athletics facility. Facilities built in the last 15 years may be more appropriate for day camps than older facilities, but you will still have to adapt in some ways to make them safe and appropriate for children. In addition to the day camp, the managing university department may also be responsible for providing ongoing services to students, faculty, staff, and other summer camps at the same time. These challenges are reviewed more fully in chapters 6 and 7 of this book.

Municipality camps make use of existing facilities like a school art room to offer quality programs for children.

Camp Dost in Pennsylvania, a program of the Danville Ronald McDonald House, is funded by the nonprofit organization and other contributions. The camp is designed so that children with cancer can have fun doing many of the same things other children their ages do.

Private Camps

Facility-based camps may also be housed in private gyms and fitness organizations that rely on revenue generated from memberships, sponsorships, or donations from the larger community. These organizations have found that providing children's programs increases revenue. Like university providers, private organizations may also face the challenge of having to modify their facilities to make them safe and appropriate for children's play and recreational pursuits.

Specialty Areas

You also need to determine the kind of camp (i.e., specialty area and subject) you will offer—understanding, of course, that you may want to incorporate activities from other specialties as well. For example, theater camps may program swim time or physical activity time to provide a break or teach theater constructs in an environment that promotes physical activity, clears the mind, and is educational. These types of experiences break the monotony of a specialty camp and make the overall program stronger and the campers' experience more satisfying.

Identifying a specialty area to help brand the camp clarifies goals, camper outcomes, and the overall benefits of the camp. Because this book addresses facility-based camps and their promotion of positive outcomes in the cognitive, social, emotional, and physical learning domains, the discussion of specialty areas

CAMP STORIES

Day Camp Overnights

Despite operating in facility-based camp programs over the last seven years, I have always tried to incorporate an overnight component when applicable. I have found that offering overnight experiences in facility-based camps is a great way to ease children into the idea of attending residential camps as they develop and serves as an appropriate gateway to outdoor activity that can expand their minds regarding outdoor recreation. Facility-based camps wishing to offer an overnight experience must embrace a paradigm that honors the social development gained from staying overnight rather than the outdoor skills that are traditionally tied to overnight camping experiences. Additionally, depending on the camp, administrators will need to make decisions about which groups will be most affected by, and would most benefit from, an overnight experience. For example, when I worked at a Midwest college university that offered day camp programs in a facility-based camp, I identified one night during the week that the fourth-grade group (nine-year-olds) would spend the night in the facility. The night was programmed to engage the campers in several programs that they were not able to engage in during the week, included down time during the evening hours, added night swim time, and included dinner and a nighttime snack. The focus of our time together was purely social and allowed children who were apprehensive about staying overnight to become comfortable because they were with adults they trusted and a group they were familiar with in a setting that was less intimidating than the outdoors. Another example of an overnight experience that I provided for day campers was when I worked for a municipality and took a group of children camping in a local park managed by the city. In this camp, I was able to offer the middle school group exposure to an overnight camping experience in a safe space managed by the city and at minimal cost because the camp program was also managed by the city. This was a great and affordable way to offer an overnight experience to day campers that incorporated outdoor living skills and exposed many of them, for the first time, to camping outside.

will be limited to sport camps versus recreational camps, and educational camps versus therapeutic camps.

Sport Camps   Sport camps focus on sport-specific skill acquisition and development. A camp may offer one sport per week such as basketball, baseball, or ice hockey, or a different sport each day or half day to expose campers to a variety of sports. Traditional sport camps that focus on only one sport, such as a basketball camp managed by a local high school or college basketball program, are also hugely popular in local communities.

Recreational Camps   Recreational camps are different from sport camps in that they aim to expose children to recreational and leisure activities they may or may not have participated in. Recreational camps tend to be less competitive and more oriented toward social interaction than sport camps are. They focus on appreciating physical activities with friends without the threat of competition. Although skill development occurs regularly in recreational camps, it is not the primary focus. Campers may be offered waterfront, adventure, and leisure activities, and many more. Recreational camps that employ themes tend to have more flexibility in what they offer from session to session. However, the more themes your facility-based camp program tries to employ, the more challenges you will face in making those themed programs successful.

Educational Camps   Some day camps are developed for educational or therapeutic purposes. Although all camps are educational in many regards, not all specifically identify educational goals. Educational camps tend to focus on specific subjects such as science, math, engineering, music, debate, political science, computers, leadership, social justice, and the arts, among others. Although campers are also learning social skills, these are secondary to the primary educational goals. Some educational camps partner with local schools to develop experiences that meet state educational requirements by providing fun, hands-on, off-campus educational events to supplement school education.

Educational camps are growing in popularity and can be easily accommodated in facility-based camps as well as program-based camps. However, in some communities the facility-based camp housed at local educational centers will have the advantage over program-based camps. This is because of the design considerations of facilities built to serve organized camping experiences versus the design considerations of educational facilities. As such, incorporating educational constructs and learning outcomes into facility-based recreational day camps housed at schools, such as leadership development, becomes a reasonable goal for camp administrators.

Therapeutic Camps   Therapeutic camps heal the mind, body, or soul of participants. They include religious camps, camps for the disabled, camps for overweight children, camps for children from same sex homes, camps for children who have been abused or neglected, and camps for terminally ill children. Therapeutic camps may offer any and all variations of overnight and day camp options, and may include sport, recreation, and leisure-time pursuits. These camps differ from the others discussed here because the mission and goals of the camp are directly linked to healing children through play and recreation. They may even include spiritual components or activities such as prayer and worship. These camps may have stricter health and safety standards or different meals and traditions than general recreational camps according to the needs of participants.

Diversity and Flexibility

Every facility-based camp is unique by virtue of the changing landscape of programs, missions, populations, facilities, and leaders. Because of this variability, you must understand the available program options. Determining the scope of programs is challenging but fun. Remaining open and flexible will help you create unique opportunities in recreation, sport, education, or therapeutic camp settings that meet the needs of your community.

Conclusion

Facility-based camps provide a useful and desired service to community members. Familiarity with the history of camping will help you understand the range and scope of opportunities camps provide. Understanding the benefits of camping will also help you create and fund your program. Facility-based camps include municipality, campus, and private camps and can serve specific specialties within these classifications. Examples of the specialties discussed in this chapter include sport camps, recreational camps, educational camps, and therapeutic camps.

The general overview provided in this chapter regarding the history of camping, benefits to children of day camps, and types of camp programs is a helpful preview for the contents, considerations, suggestions, and resources offered in subsequent chapters. Chapter 2 provides more specific tools for assessing community needs, identifying funding sources, and developing a plan for branding and marketing your camp program.

Getting Started

If you are looking to implement a new camp program in an existing facility, you may be unsure about what the camp should look like, how it should run, how to offer it to the community, and what the outcomes of the camp should be. If you are running an existing program and looking to revitalize your offerings, you may also have difficulty determining which programs should stay, which should go, and which should be reconstructed. In either case, understanding your community and your available resources is crucial to making good decisions. This chapter presents strategies for finding the information you need to make these decisions.

This chapter begins by addressing the need to survey the community to learn what constituents are looking for in a camp. The next step is to identify available resources within your organization and the surrounding community. You should also invest sufficient time in researching the pulse of today's camping world. Decisions about the operation of the camp and its programs must then be translated into action steps. Finally, you must articulate those decisions as a camp mission and camp goals.

Community Survey

Before anything else happens, you must identify the needs of the community your camp program will serve. Understanding national trends and best practices in camp programs is important, and that will be outlined later. At this point, you need to secure community buy-in, which is essential to the success of any program. Additionally, community relationships formed during this process send a strong message to the members at large that you are in tune with the community's needs, and these relationships will help sustain your camp over the long term.

If you are cringing as you read the word *survey*, you may be heartened to learn that there are several ways to administer surveys so that they are not intrusive to the community, do not require a large amount of time, and can be easily analyzed.

Additionally, interpreting the data does not have to result in a massive headache if you consider yourself data illiterate. In fact, the collected variables can be easy to understand and will provide a great deal of information.

Basic Considerations

Surveying the community entails three basic considerations. The first, and perhaps most difficult, is determining the type, scope, and length of the questionnaire. In other words, what instrument should you use? Second, you need to establish criteria or a selection process for identifying who will complete the survey. Third, you will want to identify the easiest, least intrusive, and most effective way to distribute the surveys to ensure an adequate response rate.

Instrument Selection

The most difficult part of conducting any survey is often determining which instrument to use. You need to find an instrument that will adequately measure the pulse of the community. If you want to ascertain a need or desire for a new camp in conjunction with the likelihood of the community's continued use of the new program, you may consider a basic market study. If you are looking to find out what people would like to see in the new program or an existing program, you may use a program needs assessment. A shorter survey would help you identify the logistical needs of the community. If you are starting a new camp program, you will most likely want data on all of these things.

Many times, existing surveys can be used with some slight modifications. Modifying a survey, however, may require permission from the survey developer, so keep that in mind when planning the timeline of survey distribution. You may find, on the other hand, that you have to develop your own survey. Either way, the instrument needs to be valid and reliable, which means that it should not include leading questions that may unintentionally skew answers and give inaccurate results.

If you are designing your own survey, begin by reviewing existing surveys to get ideas about questions that are appropriate for your community and how to word them. You also should have a human reference (a knowledgeable colleague that can provide some guidance during the process) and a physical resource (such as a sample survey from said colleague) to ensure adequate instrument development as you go through the process.

Following is a short list of web sites that offer community needs assessment guides that might be helpful:

- www.ncstac.org/content/materials/CommunityNeedsAssessment.pdf
- www.smartlemming.com/category/smart-lemming-toolkit/
- www.communityaction.org/files/HigherGround/Community_Needs_Assessment_Tool_Kit.pdf
- www.dpi.state.nd.us/grants/needs.pdf
- www.luc.edu/curl/pdfs/A_Community_Needs_Assessment_Guide_.pdf

 In addition, the CD-ROM includes a template for developing a needs assessment instrument (form 2.1: Needs Assessment Survey).

FORM 2.1

Needs Assessment Survey

To ascertain community interest in and support of a new summer day camp program for children, we would like your feedback regarding administrative components, scheduling, and program options. Please take a few minutes to complete this survey. Indicate to what extent you agree (strongly agree, SA; agree, A; neutral, N; strongly disagree, SD) with the following statements:

_____ The community needs a summer day camp program for children ages 5 to 14.
_____ The camp program should offer pay-over-time options.
_____ The camp program should offer sibling discounts.
_____ The camp program should offer an online registration process.
_____ The camp program should offer a mail-in registration process.
_____ The camp program should offer a walk-in registration process.
_____ The camp program should offer care for children between 9 a.m. and 5 p.m.
_____ A reasonable price for this service would be between $125 and $180 per week.
_____ I would be willing to pay that amount per week to send my child to camp.
_____ The camp program should offer an early care option from 7 a.m. to 9 a.m.
_____ A reasonable price for this service would be between $10 and $15 per week.
_____ I would be willing to pay that amount per week for early care.
_____ The camp program should offer extended care from 5 p.m. to 6 p.m.
_____ A reasonable price for this service would be between $5 and $10 per week.
_____ I would be willing to pay that amount per week for extended care.
_____ The most important thing about a summer camp program is safety.
_____ Having staff with certifications relevant to child care is necessary.
_____ Staff should have at least one year of experience working with children.
_____ Staff should be 18 or older.

Please rate the following programs (1 is the program you would most like to see in a day camp program and the highest number represents the program you would least be interested to see in a day camp program).

_____ Arts and crafts _____ Performance arts
_____ Sports and games _____ Team building
_____ All-camp program _____ Informal play
_____ Fitness fun _____ Nature/environmental science
_____ Wall climbing _____ Outdoor adventure/recreation
_____ Archery _____ Clubs

From J. Moffit, 2011, Day camp programming and administration: Core skills and practices (Champaign, IL: Human Kinetics). Adapted, by permission, from University of North Carolina, Asheville Campus Recreation.

Quantitative methods of data collection provide a numerical picture of the general needs of the community (e.g., a majority of respondents are in favor of an extended care camp program). Qualitative methods, on the other hand, reveal the bigger picture, such as why people need extended care and how long the extended care should be to accommodate that need. Qualitative analyses may require the use of focus groups, individual interviews, case studies, or observations. Although this type of data collection can be useful, it requires much more time because it involves engaging in relationships or developing new ones. Furthermore, the interpretation of the data, although seemingly less confusing than statistical analysis, can take up to five times longer.

In summation, determining the instrument to use for your community assessment depends on the information you want. Take advantage of the literature and develop a body of knowledge by reviewing existing instruments before developing a new one. Modifying an existing survey may be the simplest way to determine the needs of your community.

Participant Selection

The demographics of the participants in your survey should fairly accurately reflect those of the larger community. This section highlights three methods of selecting participants to achieve this goal. First, and most effective, is to randomly select participants from the community and invite them to participate. Second, you may choose participants out of convenience if you know people who are willing to take the survey and you believe they can provide good, honest feedback. Your third choice is to send the survey out to every community member. You may also decide that other options such as case studies, focus groups, or interviews are more appropriate for your organization.

Random Sampling Random sampling of participants ensures a representative sample of the larger community. Data from a randomly selected subject population

CAMP STORIES

Modifying Existing Instruments

In my work as a camp practitioner across various camp types and recreational sectors and in several U.S. locations, I have found that modifying existing instruments gives me the time to adjust to and advocate for a new community. It provides more time to build relationships as I focus on what existing research recommends and ascertain the needs of the community. I generally engage in qualitative methods after forging relationships with parents and children, which has allowed me to achieve community buy-in and sell the long-term vision of the camp program to organizational leaders on whom I depend for continued support. The final advantage of using a preexisting instrument is that I can be assured of the instrument's reliability and validity because someone in the field has already determined these qualities.

tend to portray the most accurate picture of the culture, climate, and pulse of the community studied, provided an appropriate response rate was achieved. Additionally, truly randomly selected subjects produce a confidence interval that adds to the value and validity of the data. In other words, randomly selected populations provide an extra assurance that the data collected are representative of the community and therefore provide quality data that can help inform your decisions about camp programming. Following is a short, and certainly not exhaustive, list of ways to randomly select community participants:

- Randomly select names from a phonebook (i.e., the point-and-call method).
- Call every third, sixth, or tenth person in the phonebook (or any number you choose).
- Randomly select names from the town or city census if available.
- Randomly select e-mail addresses from town or city public records if available.
- For a new program in the public or private sector, find names, e-mail addresses, or home addresses in the organization's current records. Then, choose a number, such as 12, and invite every 12th person on the list to participate in the survey.

Convenience Sampling   The second method of choosing survey participants is convenience sampling. Convenience sampling is predicated on the fact that administrators would choose individuals to take the survey. Individuals selected to complete the survey typically already have a relationship with the camp practitioner or the larger organization. Selecting individuals may involve the practitioner reaching out to people he or she knows and can count on to give honest feedback, or it can be convenient in that the practitioner decides to put the survey at a central location where many patrons of the organization will congregate. The practitioner would then ask patrons as they enter the communal space to take the survey. This method of convenience sampling does not hinge on the relationships of the practitioners, but it does rely on the patrons' relationship to the larger organization. A benefit of convenience sampling beyond time considerations is that individuals asked to take the survey can, and often do, encourage their circle of friends to take the survey. This is known as a snowball effect and brings added value to the data collected. Although this method may not be as representative of the larger community as a random sampling, it provides high-quality data from constituents that the organization is already serving. In this way, it may provide the most useful and practical data on which to base decisions. In the end, the programs offered must match the needs of the people for whom they were created.

Convenience sampling is generally quick, easy, and effective in ascertaining the needs of the community the camp program will serve. For this reason, it is recommended over random sampling because it minimizes the time you will have to spend conducting the survey in addition to your other duties. Moreover, convenience sampling generally results in a high response rate because those completing the survey are usually interested in the services offered. Although this method is not the most scientific approach to data collection, it is the most applicable to the work and goals of camp professionals.

Community-Wide Sampling   The third participant selection option is to distribute the survey to every member of the community. Although doing so invites a large number of responses, the responses may not be meaningful enough to facilitate good decision making. Although you may receive a high number of responses from a community-wide survey, you may have difficulty knowing whether the data are representative of the larger community or of the population you are serving or hope to serve. The data gathered from this method can be very enlightening and descriptive but highly variable. This can make determining your camp program direction problematic. Prioritizing your needs in terms of time limitations and resources required to distribute the survey is essential when using the community-wide sampling method. In other words, you will want to identify which community members will provide the most meaningful feedback to make decisions regarding your camp program. For example, if you live in a large municipality and are looking to start a camp in a particular grid of the city, then the community whose needs you will be most concerned about are the members who are most likely to attend your camp based on its location. In this example, you would identify that community and send out a community-wide survey rather than sending a survey to every member of the larger population.

The value of the community-wide sampling method lies in the unexpected data it can elicit. Learning about the populations the camp doesn't serve and how it excludes them can be incredibly valuable for existing programs. Also, identifying community needs that you did not initially consider can be very helpful in planning a camp program. On the other hand, if your survey reveals a lack of interest in the camp altogether, this is good to know prior to making an investment of time, money, and resources that could be better spent elsewhere.

For existing camps, surveying the entire camp population is invaluable for ascertaining their evolving needs. Distributing the survey prior to the start of camp, rather than at the end of the camp season, distinguishes this method as

Community surveys can help you identify the needs of the community you will serve. For example, the results of your survey could indicate that many in the community would be interested in horse-riding lessons.

a needs assessment rather than an evaluation and can help you make decisions going into the current camp season.

Survey Distribution

The way you distribute surveys can mean the difference between hitting the necessary response rate and not hitting it. The bottom line is that you want to make sure that participants can quickly and conveniently return their completed surveys. Many surveys are conducted by mail, by phone, and on site. These methods are valid but are not ideal if you have little time, little money, and a quickly approaching deadline. E-mail surveys have several time and economic advantages over these other methods. Most convenient, however, may be online, web-based surveys.

Mail-in surveys require that the instrument be sent out and returned to the organization. A cover letter describes the survey purpose and typically asks the respondent to complete the survey and mail it back using a pre-stamped, self-addressed envelope. Although some respondents may be receptive to this, many likely will not. As a result, you may spend a great deal of money on copying and postage with no guarantee that the surveys will be returned by the stated deadline. Additionally, mail-in surveys require that you organize the data of each survey by hand. This is time-consuming, and given that the response rate may be low, it is hardly worth the effort.

Phone interviews are good if they take less than five minutes. Anything longer will ultimately annoy participants, and the result may be a curt line disconnection midsurvey. Furthermore, transcribing the data of phone surveys and then organizing them can be time-consuming. Finally, if you are planning to do short phone interviews of survey participants after they have responded, the initial survey method should not be via phone. Follow-up interviews may be necessary if the practitioner gleans something from the phone survey data that requires more detail or that the practitioner would like to learn more about to help further guide decision making.

On-site survey distribution can facilitate random selection because whoever shows up is asked to complete the survey. However, ascertaining bias is difficult with this method because those who already participate are showing up regularly. Because you can assume that respondents are already vested in the organization, you should use the results cautiously. Also, organizing the responses and data of on-site surveys requires a great deal of time because it must be done by hand.

E-mail survey distribution is convenient on several fronts. First, it allows you to randomly or conveniently choose participants from e-mail lists you may already have. Second, participants can complete the survey immediately upon receiving the e-mail and send it back quickly. This helps create a good response rate. Third, the data collected are submitted and stored electronically, so you simply have to copy and paste to organize them. Finally, the cost, in both time and money, is low

Online survey distribution is the most convenient method for participants and will likely result in higher participation numbers. With a larger number of responses, you may determine the desire exists for a program to teach or improve computer skills.

for both you and participants. You lose nothing in time or money when people choose not to respond, and e-mails cause little disruption in people's lives.

The final method of survey distribution discussed here, and the one recommended, is via online tools. This entails sending an e-mail inviting participants to go to a web site to complete the survey. At the end of the survey, the participant selects Submit, and the data are automatically stored in an online database that you have set up. This creates minimal disruption and annoyance for survey participants, is easy to navigate using current technology, and does not require you to organize individual surveys.

Acquiring e-mail addresses may be difficult if you are starting up a new camp program. Consider partnering with community schools or the local parks and recreation department, because they tend to have access to a large number of

CAMP COUNSEL

Survey Distribution

Regardless of your survey distribution method, consider offering community members an incentive for completing the survey by the deadline, such as the following:

- Discount on monthly membership
- Discount on camp registration
- Gift certificate to be used toward any of the organization's programs
- Free apparel and other merchandise the organization sells

Don't be afraid to follow up via telephone or e-mail with nonrespondents to encourage a higher response rate. Consider the following:

- Sending a reminder to nonrespondents at least one week prior to the deadline can help you reach a higher response rate (at this stage they may still respond, and this is always better than having to follow up).
- Following up with nonrespondents provides another opportunity to solicit feedback.
- Following up with nonrespondents also provides insight into why some community members would participate in the camp program and some would not.
- Reach out to nonrespondents only once. Remember, participation is voluntary.

Include a cover letter with any survey that explains the following:

- The purpose of the survey
- How long it will take to complete
- Any incentives you are offering for survey completion
- Instructions for completing the survey
- A reminder that participation is voluntary

families. Because many facility-based camps grow from these organizations, you may already have access to the larger organization's e-mail database.

Typically, online surveys are more expensive than other types, but the time, effort, and annoyance they save make them well worth the cost. Several online survey hosts provide free trials or free access, depending on the capabilities the camp wishes to use. For example, Survey Monkey (www.surveymonkey.com) and Zoomerrang (www.zoomerrang.com) provide online survey tools, data organization, and distribution methods that are affordable and effective. The tools they offer also help organizations evaluate camp programs and other programs throughout the year, so their fees are quite reasonable. Most universities already have survey software that collects and stores data and that is free to students, faculty, and staff.

Data Analysis and Interpretation

Many recreation professionals dislike or even fear the process of data analysis. The profession is generally more comfortable basing programming decisions on patron feedback, specifically verbal feedback, and on current trends in the field, rather than on crunching numbers, identifying themes, and analyzing factors. However, interpreting data for the purpose of camp programming is important and relatively easy.

This section reviews three methods for analyzing data: quantitative methods, qualitative methods, and triangulation. The final section provides a sample of how to organize the data into a strategic plan. Note that these methods were selected based on their implementation potential for the working recreational professional; this section is not intended to be an exhaustive list of data analysis methods.

Quantitative Methods

Quantitative methods for data interpretation are varied, may seem confusing, and tend to cause people the most grief. Data from all quantitative methods are analyzed using numbers. In quantitative analysis, the researcher asks a question, gathers the answers, and then makes assumptions based on the numerical descriptions that are generated through analysis. Of course, the analysis method employed will affect the types of assumptions made, so it's important to remember that quantitative methods are not always about just numbers. Some argue that they can be just as subjective as qualitative methods if the statistical measure used to analyze the data does not match the goal of the question. The bottom line is that understanding which statistical tests to run and why provides more meaningful results to base decisions on. This may be the primary reason that descriptive statistical tests are the most commonly used among recreation professionals.

Descriptive statistics provide a detailed picture of the who, what, when, how, and why of recreation services. These measurements are important in showcasing an organization's growth in participation patterns, participation numbers, demographics (e.g., old, young, male, female, black, white, transgender), and financial situation. If you want to determine the needs of the community, descriptive statistics will be incredibly useful. If numbers are not enough, you may wish to employ data analysis methods to get a more rounded picture for any given question. If this is the case, then supplement descriptive statistics with some of the qualitative methods for data interpretation discussed next.

Qualitative Methods

Researchers using qualitative methods interpret the data, interviews, documents, materials, or literature to make assumptions about given phenomena. For this reason, some scholars argue that qualitative methods lack the objectivity of quantitative methods because one cannot misinterpret numbers. Both methods are valuable, however, because they provide different types of information that are useful during the decision-making process. More often than not, the decision to use quantitative methods over qualitative methods boils down to time. Surveys conducted using qualitative methods, no matter how valuable, can take up to five times longer to conduct and analyze than those conducted using quantitative methods, depending on the scope of the questions and the size of the sample.

Triangulation

If you have enough time to interpret qualitative data, you must begin the daunting task of triangulation. One way to make qualitative data interpretation less biased is to examine several pieces of the question and compare the results. Data that are not solicited through "hard science" methods become more valuable when triangulated. Keep that in mind when presenting data and results to any organizational authority that must support any initiative for camp programming.

For example, if you want to implement a payment plan for your patrons but are unsure whether the plan would be well received by families and fiscally sound for the camp, you could use triangulation to inform your decision (see figure 2.1). Triangulation is not necessarily a linear process, but for simplicity's sake, the following example will walk you through the process linearly. First, you solicit feedback from past and returning participants through informal conversations, focus groups, or individual interviews, all of which require excellent notes. You then transcribe the interviews (plan for four hours of transcription for every one-hour interview) and identify common themes among the participants. You discover that one of the themes that emerged from the participant dialogues is that the community indicate they can't afford to pay up front for multiple children attending multiple weeks like the current camp policy requires.

Next, you run reports from the registration software (or compile reports from documented registration procedures) that identify how many families paid for the full price of camp at registration and how many specifically asked for a payment plan. You supplement this report with additional reports that describe when families registered. For instance, if most participants registered and made full payment on a Friday (typically a payday), you might assume that a payment plan is warranted so people could register whenever they wish and pay over time.

Finally, you gather payment policy information from other area camps and examine current trends to see where your camp falls on the continuum. If your camp stands alone by not offering a payment plan, it could be argued that it is not keeping up with the competition and is losing potential campers. If no other camps have payment plans, no action may be necessary because the camp is operating well within industry standards.

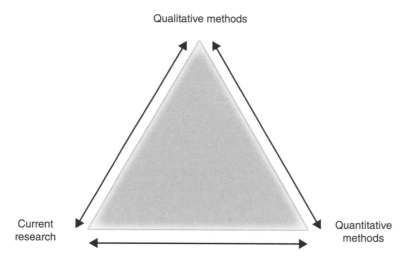

Figure 2.1 When analyzing data through triangulation for the example described in the text, qualitative methods are used via focus groups (top of the triangle) and compared to quantitative numbers (right bottom of the triangle) from a survey instrument before being compared to the current research and best practices in the field (left bottom of the triangle). Triangulation analysis is used to get a well-rounded picture of the needs of the community based on three variables to facilitate decision making about programming.

Organizing the Data

Regardless of which method you use to gather and interpret data, the most important thing to remember is to be steadfast and consistent so that the data are representative of the community and will therefore help you make informed decisions about camp programming. Once you have analyzed all the data, it is time to start organizing them to help you synthesize the key results (see table 2.1).

Camp Inventory

Once the data from the survey have been analyzed and organized, the next step is to determine the camp's resources. An inventory of the organization's means as well as the means of the surrounding community is essential in determining if and at what level the camp can provide services.

Space and Facilities

The camp inventory includes establishing how much space will be available to participants and the times of day facilities can be used. Facility-based camps are often limited to programming activities around available times, which can create a camp day that is not ideal for children of a certain age. Although this may seem like merely a practical consideration, your program is trying to establish a reputation. The time of day five-year-olds eat, swim, and play sports affects their overall experience and can ultimately affect the reputation of the

Table 2.1 Organized Data of Community Feedback

Response %	Ages served	Programs	Times	Registration preference	Payment plans	Field trips	Outcomes
<10	1-4	Innovative games Team building Science programs	8 a.m.-12 p.m.	Walk-in	Monthly plan	Daily	Learn physical or cognitive skills
>50	5-10	Sports and games Archery Swim lessons Outdoor recreation Adventure	8 a.m.-4 p.m.	Online	Deposit plan, then full payment by June 1	Biweekly	Safety Fun Learning Meet new friends Manage emotions
<20	11-13	Environmental science Nature	8 a.m.-5 p.m.	Mail-in		Weekly	Prepare for school
<9	14-17	Horseback riding Sailing Leaders in training Counselors in training	9 a.m.-1 p.m.	Phone	Pay in full	Never	Become skilled athlete

camp. So, if at all possible, advocate for prime times in the facility you are using.

For example, if you want to schedule swim lessons and free swim for your campers from 11 a.m. to 2 p.m., and the facility you use has a regular guest swim from noon to 1 p.m., you may meet some resistance. Try to negotiate this time with conditions to get a lock on the space at that time of day for the majority of the camp season. You might negotiate an arrangement in which the youngest campers swim from 11 a.m. to 12:30 p.m., before lunch. The advantage for the camp is also an advantage for the organization, because it minimizes the number of accidents in the pool that the youngest campers can have, especially after lunch. Treating the pool after these incidents is expensive and closes the pool down for days, affecting everyone's use.

In return for that prime time during the camp season, you should allow extra time for other pool patrons and be willing to communicate the changes in the summer pool schedule to regular patrons. Communicating ahead of time and collaborating with coworkers and patrons in advance minimizes any hard feelings or miscommunication that may arise from scheduling conflicts during the camp season.

In addition to considering facility needs and resources, you should draw up a list of activities that can be accommodated in each of the areas the camp has access to. Generally, multipurpose spaces arc ideal for facility-based camps because they can accommodate a wide range of activities.

Multipurpose spaces are valuable because of the wide variety of activities that could be done in them.

A final, and most important, consideration in your space inventory is determining the safety concerns and preventive measures that the space invites. If the space is not safe for children's activities, determine whether it can be changed or cleaned up to become a safe play area—or whether it should be used at all given the potential risk.

Equipment

Once you have identified the space and the activities that the space can accommodate, the next phase of the planning process is to determine your equipment needs. Begin with an inventory of equipment already used by the organization, and ask the following questions:

- How much of the organization's equipment is available for camp use?
- How safe is the equipment in general?
- Is the equipment safe for children?
- Can currently damaged equipment be repaired for camp use?
- How much will it cost to repair damaged equipment?

If you are sharing facilities and programs, you may need to request permission to use existing equipment. The organization may require a usage fee in the case of damage to or loss of equipment. Be sure to factor these issues into your equipment inventory.

Facility and Space Modifications

To offer more varied recreational, sport, and leisure-time activities in a facility not intended for camp use, you may have to consider room or space modifications. Does the facility have a space that can be reasonably converted into an arts and crafts, nature, or environmental awareness space? A reasonable makeover may include protecting the floor and walls and providing temporary storage for supplies such as those required for arts and crafts.

The facility hosting your camp may be holding fitness programs, mind-body classes, or educational seminars in the space you are interested in using. These programs may be easily accommodated in another part of the building for a limited time during the summer. For example, a multipurpose room used for summer fitness programs such as yoga or kickboxing could be held in a gym or racquetball court for the duration of the camp program. Because these changes may not be ideal for your host organization or other teachers using the space, be prepared to advocate for your needs and work hard to help other programs meet their goals. As in the pool example, you should give plenty of time for others to adjust to the changes you are requesting and help them troubleshoot any problems that may arise prior to the start of camp.

Staffing

Determining your staffing requirements is always an estimate in the planning stages. For new programs in particular, this can create challenges. First of all, you may underestimate your needs in an effort to keep costs low. Your justification may be that because the program is new, the number of campers may be low. Although this is sound logic and may be true for many programs, when it comes to camp programs, you should always expect the unexpected. On the other hand, overestimating your staffing requirements by thinking that the new program will be hugely successful may be too optimistic and could put you in a financial pickle. Instead, estimate your staffing needs based on the community feedback you received and your inventory of space and equipment.

For example, let's say that your community overwhelmingly indicated an interest in a day camp serving children ages 6 to 10. Assuming that your camp will serve five age groups within this range is an adequate starting point for determining your staffing needs. Keep in mind that the recommended counselor-to-camper ratio in a facility-based camp is 1:10 (this differs from the ACA recommendation of 1:15). A low estimate of participation for a new camp is 12 participants per group, for a total of 60 participants. In this example, you would need six counselors.

Now you must consider a more optimistic number of participants. A high estimate is 20 participants per group, for a total of 100 participants. This number would require 10 counselors to maintain the ratio. Your safest bet would be to plan for the average of the high and low numbers: 80 participants for a total of eight counselors.

Eight counselors is a reasonable starting point. However, keep in mind that this is merely a working estimate that should be updated as the process continues. Ultimately, the number of counselors you hire will depend on the final number of participants who enroll. You must be comfortable working in this type of ambiguity, at least for a while. Developing a proper timeline and strategic plan should give you plenty of time to increase or decrease your staff numbers as the number of campers fluctuates throughout the process.

If you find that you have hired too many counselors, and you have no desire to keep enrollment open, you have three options: keep all the counselors you hired, find other positions for some of them, or terminate some of them.

If you decide to retain the extra counselors, you can create a daily schedule that staggers when counselors are on duty. This gives counselors a more manageable workweek: some days they will work six hours, and others they will work eight. A schedule that varies from week to week is another option. Counselors may appreciate the rotating schedule as the summer progresses because working with children is not easy. The key is to set the schedule at the beginning of the summer so that counselors can plan accordingly. If, instead, you change the schedule frequently, the counselors may appreciate the concept, but they won't appreciate you. A rotating schedule also gives you some flexibility in scheduling time off or arranging for counselors to leave for doctor appointments and other personal reasons. Make it clear that all personal needs should be scheduled around the rotating schedule posted at the beginning of the camp season. Finally, a rotating schedule allows you to change the schedule easily when staff emergencies and illnesses happen. Most staff understand the need to fill in during an emergency or illness.

Your second option if you find yourself overstaffed is to find other positions in other parts of the organization for the weakest staff members. In keeping with your commitment to these staffers, be sure to maintain the wage and number of hours per week that you promised them when you hired them. The advantage to the organization is that it sidesteps the interviewing and prescreening process required for finding additional staff. You may not be able to make these staffing shifts until after the first week of camp, at which point it will be clear which new-hires do not make the best counselors, and which are finding that working with children is not as fun as they thought it would be. Shifting staff members around isn't ideal, but a mistake in hiring can be salvaged with minimal effect on the camp, the staff members, and the organization at large.

Your third option if you have overhired staff is to terminate some of them. This is not ideal, but it is possible. The camp certainly has a right to terminate employees whenever necessary. Your best plan is to clarify with staff members from the start that job placement is contingent on the camp's needs, passing background checks, and the hours available.

Surrounding Environment

You will also want to research the surrounding community. If your program is taking place on a college or university campus, this means determining what other campus departments, offices, or resources may be useful to your program. Decide how partnerships can be formed with other campus members to serve the community's needs and desires. For example, the astronomy department may have fun learning activities that can be part of the camp experience—maybe even a planetarium. If so, establish a relationship with the department to develop activities for your camp.

Keep in mind that other campus departments may also have to generate revenue, so you may have to pay for their services. Typically, campus departments offer services at cost to other departments, so the cost could be minimal. However, it is always a good idea to see whether you can obtain services at no cost or negotiate a trade to keep the expenses for both departments low. Recent literature indicates that youth and family programs offered at a college are extremely valuable to campus enrollment managers for two reasons. First, they allow contact with youth and families early and over time, which creates an opportunity for the family to become early fans of the university. Second, research indicates that when youth have a positive experience before reaching college age, they are likely to consider those colleges when they are selecting institutions of higher education (Dennis, 2006).

If your host organization is a municipality or private organization, using the organization's resources at cost or on a trade basis will also benefit the camp, the campers, and your bottom line. Community businesses are likely to work with local camps because of the potential for additional marketing opportunities in the town (in the case of municipality camps) or the town and surrounding areas (in the case of camps run by private fitness organizations). For example, a town may ask a local indoor skate club if they can bring their campers to the park at no cost or at a reduced price. In return, the town offers the skate club space on the registration materials (printed or online) in which to market the club. This is a win–win situation, because the club does not have to spend money to advertise to a broader community, and if the cost is reduced, will still be getting some money for the services provided. The town is able to provide a fun activity at a reduced rate in exchange for only some space on the registration materials.

Table 2.2 provides an example of a camp resource inventory that includes all of the needs described in this section.

Table 2.2 Resource Inventory

Space	Times	Activities accommodated	Equipment	Needed equipment	Community partnerships	Staffing
Multipurpose gym	8 a.m.-1 p.m.	Sports and games Innovative games Archery	Baseball bats, balls, bases Jump ropes Basketballs Kickballs	Playground kits Archery arrows, bows, targets, nets	Climbing services Boating services Hiking services Ropes course (adventure program)	8 total
Pool	12 p.m.-5 p.m.	Free swim Swim lessons	Life jackets	Life jackets Noodles Beach balls Floaters	Astronomy department Geography department (Nature/environmental science features)	
Outdoor field	8 a.m.-3 p.m.	Sports and games Archery	Soccer balls Nets Lacrosse equipment Field hockey equipment		Planetariums Campus theaters Local museums Local factories	
Multipurpose studio/room	8 a.m.-12 a.m. 2 p.m.-4 p.m.	Nature Environmental science		Nature activities Environmental science	Fun parks (accommodate field trips)	

Market Analysis

In addition to knowing the community resources, you should also investigate competing camps. The importance of researching local and national trends in the field of camping cannot be overemphasized, but keep in mind that final decisions regarding camp programming should be geared toward the community you are serving. However, researching camps on a larger scale provides information that is crucial to the design of the overall camp program.

Find out what other community camps are offering in terms of programs, payment plans, and registration. Understanding what is offered and what seems to work in the community is a great way to ascertain what the community is participating in as well as to determine in what ways your camp will differ. These differences will help inform marketing strategies and methods for spreading the news about your camp program and building a reputation for sustainable growth over the next five years.

Researching current trends in camping nationwide provides general information regarding what programming is hot and what is not. This information will inform your decisions about programming and marketing and help you build a high-quality program that is competitive on a local and national scale. Additionally, researching on a larger scale also provides great ideas for your own program. Make sure that you organize your research results in a meaningful and systematic way.

Finally, make sure that the programs you offer—despite being research based— are tailored to the needs of the community you are serving. Broader research provides some certainty that your programs are current and outcome oriented and will generally be well received. Next, use the method of triangulation in figure 2.1 to begin weaving in the needs of your community. In other words, use the data collected from the community, the data gathered through the inventory, and the data collected in the market analysis to triangulate the findings and determine your program offerings. Table 2.3 offers an example of how to compile all of the data collected to compare (triangulate) findings to make camp programming decisions.

Program Decisions

After surveying the community, taking a camp inventory, and completing supplementary research through a market analysis, you should be in a good position to begin making decisions about the activities and organization of the camp day. In addition to this information, rely on the triangulated analysis to help determine what programs the camp can easily offer to the community.

Based on the information compiled in tables 2.1, 2.2, and 2.3, you may decide to offer the following:

- Sports and games
- Swimming
- Outdoor recreation

Table 2.3 Compiled Data for Program Decisions

Response %	Ages served	Programs	Times	Registration preference	Payment plans	Field trips	Outcomes
COMMUNITY INFORMATION							
<10	1-4	Innovative games Team building Science programs	8 a.m.-12 p.m.	Walk-in	Monthly plan	Daily	Learn physical or cognitive skills
>50	5-10	Sports and games Archery Swim lessons Outdoor recreation Adventure	8 a.m.-4 p.m.	Online	Deposit plan, then full payment by June 1	Biweekly	Safety Fun Learning Meet new friends Manage emotions
<20	11-13	Environmental science Nature	8 a.m.-5 p.m.	Mail-in		Weekly	Prepare for school
<9	14-17	Horseback riding Sailing Leaders in training Counselors in training	9 a.m.-1 p.m.	Phone	Pay in full	Never	Become skilled athlete
COMPETITOR INFORMATION							
<9	1-4	Beach programs Horseback Sailing	8 a.m.-12 p.m.	Phone	Monthly plan	Weekly	Cheap day care
>20	5-10	Sports and games Swim lessons Outdoor recreation Adventure	8 a.m.-4 p.m.	Walk-in	Deposit plan, then full payment by June 1	Daily	Prepare for school
<50	11-13	Environmental science Nature Archery	8 a.m.-5 p.m.	Mail-in/ online	Sibling discount	Biweekly	Safety Fun Learning
<10	14-17	Horseback riding Sailing Leaders in training Counselors in training	9 a.m.-1 p.m.	E-mail	Pay in full	Never	Become skilled athlete
NATIONAL TRENDS							
<10	1-4		8 a.m.-12 p.m.		Government subsidized	Daily	
>50	5-10	Sports and games Archery Swim lessons Outdoor recreation Adventure Innovative games Team building Science programs	8 a.m.-4 p.m.	Online	Deposit plan, then full payment by June 1	Weekly	Safety Fun Learning
<50	11-13	Environmental science Nature	8 a.m.-5 p.m.	Mail-in	Monthly plan	Weekly	
<30	14-17	Horseback riding Sailing Leaders in training Counselors in training	9 a.m.-7 p.m.	Phone	Pay in full	Daily	Become skilled athlete

- Innovative games
- Adventure
- Online registration
- Payment plan

Account for the needs of the community by determining to offer the following:

- Weekly field trips (a compromise between daily and biweekly to accommodate 80 percent of the respondents)
- Camp day from 8 a.m. to 5 p.m. (to accommodate 70 percent of the respondents)
- Archery
- Environmental science
- Nature

You now have a blueprint for your camp based on the data you collected. Now, you must determine whether it is realistic based on your inventory of resources and the financial considerations and strategic direction of the camp, as explained in the following sections.

After collecting and analyzing the data, you can determine whether to offer activities such as paddling. Your decision will also be based on other factors, including availability of resources, financial considerations, and the camp's strategic direction.

Financial Considerations

The next step is to determine the financial implications of offering camp programming. Using the previous steps, you should be able to do this relatively easily if you have updated the information during the process. Combining the data from table 2.1 with table 2.2 will reveal a working financial blueprint (see figure 2.2). It will require some tweaking and modification, but for the most part, the new table in figure 2.2 will help you determine the costs associated with your camp.

Once the financial blueprint is complete, keep in mind that it will change. This is especially true because moving forward in the planning process requires that you make decisions that will alter the face of the plans. This is normal and good. Remember that working in a facility-based camp requires a high level of flexibility in every stage of programming.

Figure 2.2 shows a sample financial blueprint. The numbers presented in the figure were calculated as follows (program expenses assume a camp that serves 80 children):

- *Wages:* $8/hour × 8 hours/day × 8 staff members × 5 days/week × 8 weeks of camp = $20,480
- *Wage fringe:* 8% (estimated fringe benefit percent paid to temp staff) × $20,480 = $1,638.40 (camps that pay for staff training have to account for this cost in the wages projection)
- *Office supplies:* Paper, pens, folders, and the cost for staff training materials estimated at $300
- *Equipment maintenance fee:* Include a maintenance fee in the cost so that you can develop a roll-over line item to replace and repair equipment when needed
- *Miscellaneous expenses:* Batteries, additional first aid needs, supplies for special events, and so on.
- *Sports and games:* Equipment needed for the program beyond that paid for with the equipment maintenance fee
- *Swimming:* Money for additional life jackets and kid-friendly pool toys and supplies
- *Archery:* Equipment needed for bows, arrows, targets, safety netting, and so on.
- *Adventure:* Programs that have to contract services can be expensive; costs will be lower or fluctuate for programs that can provide services in house or on campus.
- *Field trips:* [Cost of transportation per hour ($45/hour) × number of buses needed (2) × length of time per trip (5 hours) × number of trips (8, one trip per week) = $3,600] + [field trip admission fees @ group rate of $4/child and $5/adult: ($4 × 80) + ($5 × 8) = $360/week × 8 weeks = $2,880] = $6,480
- *Nature:* Equipment needed (magnifying glasses, jars, plants, nets, pens and paper; these materials can also be used for environmental science, depending on lesson plans)

FINANCIAL PLAN

EXPENSES			INCOME		
	Projected	Actual		Projected	Actual
Wages	$20,480		Week 1	$8,400.00	
Wage fringe	$1,638.40		Week 2	$8,400.00	
Office supplies	$300.00		Week 3	$8,400.00	
Equipment maintenance fee	$300.00		Week 4	$8,400.00	
Miscellaneous expenses	$500.00		Week 5	$8,400.00	
Sports and games	$1,000.00		Week 6	$8,400.00	
Swimming	$200.00		Week 7	$8,400.00	
Archery	$1,500.00		Week 8	$8,400.00	
Adventure	$2,000.00				
Field trips	$6,480.00				
Nature	$500.00				
Environmental science	$500.00				
Marketing	$2,000.00				
Camp shirts or other gear	$650.00				
Total	$38,048.40		Total	$67,200.00	

Income	$67,200.00	
Expenses	$38,048.40	
Profit	$29,151.60	

Other (Optional) Expenses to Consider

Snacks

$1.00/snack/kid = $2.00/kid/day = 10.00/kid/week + 20% profit = $12/kid/week

Start-Up Costs for Online Registration

The cost of setting up an account with a company that provides online registration for organizations will range between $250 and $1,000 depending on the company and the software capability.

Service fees that the camp will owe the company for processing registration will be between 7 and 12 percent of the total fee for each transaction (this cost can be built into the total cost of the camp for families).

Software for the full organization (programs and departments split the cost) would range between $2,000 and $16,000 depending on the scope and capability of the software.

A full software package would range between $8,000 and $80,000 depending on the scope and capability of the software.

Figure 2.2 The financial plan was derived based on the examples used in this chapter that were compiled in tables 2.1 and 2.2 to give practitioners an idea of how these assessments merge into a fiscal blueprint for the summer camp program.

- *Environmental science:* Equipment needed (Leave No Trace educational materials, pens, paper)
- *Marketing:* New programs need to be willing to spend more; existing programs can typically get away with using 75 percent of the initial marketing allocation.
- *Camp shirts or other gear:* These are perks that you provide for free to campers. Gear is a great marketing tool because it can be worn outside of camp, potentially all year long. Order 100 shirts at an average cost of $5.75/shirt = $575 + shipping @ ~$75 (high estimate) = $650.
- *Camp income:* Estimated total cost of camp ($38,048.40) / number of weeks (8) / number of campers per week (80) = 59.45 base cost of camper per week + 80% profit per child (47.56) = $107.01 per camper per week + $15.00/kid for miscellaneous and unexpected costs = $122.01. For marketing purposes, round up, so campers will pay $125.00 per week to attend this camp. The goal is to get 80 campers, but plan for not hitting that number by estimating your income for the camp low. See figure 2.2.

Keep in mind this is a baseline number, based on the market analysis completed, so you may determine to charge up to a 100-percent profit margin per child and still be well within market competition (in this case, the cost of camp would be between $135.00 and $140.00 per camper). Your profit margin will depend on the economic needs of your community and organization. Depending on the geographical location of the camp, this may still be well within market value. If not, you will need to cut expenses. This may be done through camp gear, field trips, and equipment or office supplies. Financial cuts should never come from wages because safety is always the most important aspect of a camp program. The counselor-to-camper ratio should be nonnegotiable considering facility based camps are extremely reliant on qualified staff to ensure the long-term sustainability of the camp.

Determining the profit percent and final camp tuition will ultimately depend on the camp, the location, the community, the expenses, and the total enrollment number. At any rate, in your financial plan you should estimate expenses high and revenue low to ensure that the camp does not lose money. Any money made over covered expenses is profit. As the camp's reputation and numbers grow over the years, so too does the profit margin. If you are starting a new program, be conservative on the estimates. For existing programs, the financial plan should mirror or closely resemble that of previous years if no increase in profit margin is necessary.

Strategic Direction

If you are looking to revitalize the programming of an existing camp, revising the strategic direction to give it new life is a helpful place to start. You might think it curious that the discussion of strategic direction appears at the end of this chapter. However, given the constraints that facility-based camps face coupled with the considerations required for developing new programs, it is fitting that strategic direction be reviewed at the end. After all, developing a direction without adequate resources or practical implementation strategies could be a monumental waste of time. For the working practitioner, this is an unacceptable annoyance.

Developing your strategic direction after all that work provides reasonable action steps because you understand the resources available and the financial implications of your camp. Knowing all of this information ahead of time makes the process of strategic development fun and exciting because you can visualize the realization of your plans. Strategic planning begins by identifying where the camp hopes to be in a predetermined amount of time and moves into the development of a mission, objectives, and an evaluation strategy.

Mission and Objectives

Where do you want your new program to be in three to five years? Is the ultimate goal to generate a certain amount of money, create a great reputation in the community, serve a particular segment of the community, have a certain number of participants, provide high-quality programs, or develop staff? Although all of these may be objectives of the camp, the ultimate goal should be the one thing the organization absolutely needs or wants to happen above all else. Once that decision is made, you can begin moving forward with a three-year strategic plan. Returning again to the sample camp discussed earlier, the ultimate goal of the

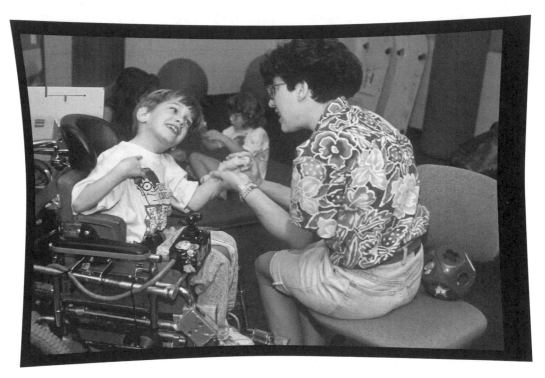

You need to know the ultimate goal of your program to develop a consistent mission statement and objectives. If your goal is to serve children with special needs, you will need to develop a mission statement and objectives that will lead you to achieve the goal.

program in three years is to have built an outstanding reputation in the community. Knowing that goal allows us to create the mission and objectives of the program.

Now it's time to unpack the ultimate goal. In this case, the following questions need to be answered before moving on:

- What does an outstanding reputation consist of?
  - Safety of campers and staff at all times
  - Trained and supported staff
  - High-quality programs
  - Varied programs
  - Dynamic scheduling
  - Exceptional customer service
  - Outstanding communication
  - Reasonable but competitive pricing
  - Easy and effective registration and payment policies
  - Learning outcomes achieved for campers and staff
- What will an outstanding reputation bring to the organization?
  - Growing population of campers from year to year to sustain the program
  - Revenue to sustain the organization
  - Greater community support
- How will the organization begin to build the reputation?
  - Ensuring safety
  - Planning
  - Organizing
  - Preparing
  - Marketing
  - Staff training
  - Offering convenient services
  - Meeting the community's needs
  - Focusing on intergenerational relationships
  - Communicating well with parents and staff at all times

The following mission and objectives were created based on the answers to the preceding questions:

Mission

Sample Day Camp strives to provide high-quality programs for young children and adolescents that foster learning, respect for others, social skills development, community living, and emotional growth in a safe, fun, physically active, and challenging environment. Sample Day Camp provides service learning opportunities to staff through hands-on training and professional, personal, and social skills development.

Objectives

1. Encourage campers to be caring, trustworthy, fair, and overall good citizens by providing a variety of opportunities in which they can experience success, constructive failure, and team collaboration.

2. Encourage campers to respect all living things and property by pointing out attitudes, words, and behaviors that are disrespectful and hurt others' feelings, others' things, or other creatures they may come into contact with during their camp experience. This will allow campers to be resilient, resourceful, and responsible.

3. Foster a group environment that encourages participation, provides leadership opportunities, and emphasizes communication by providing team-building challenges.

4. Teach campers how to balance their interdependence with others with their desire to be independent so that they are equipped to decide how to meet their emotional needs.

5. Provide campers opportunities for success by teaching them to do new things, and help them master physical skills through creative, innovative, and varied programs.

Action Steps

Developing a mission and objectives is not enough. Now it's time to determine how the program will achieve its goals over the next summer and over the next three summers. These will become the action steps that get the camp from point A to point B and will be largely informed by the resources inventoried and by the objectives of the camp. However, generally speaking, new programs should follow at least seven general action steps (see figure 2.3). These steps are discussed next, with the understanding that the details will look very different from camp to camp.

First, for a new camp, you must figure out how to market the program. This requires a marketing strategy. Refer to the market analysis you conducted and look into the internal resources of the larger organization to create a marketing plan.

Second, the camp must implement all of the logistical and financial plans developed during the planning process. You created these plans for a reason, and although you may experience some stumbles in the implementation process, it's important to give the plan a chance by allowing it to develop fully during its implementation phase. This may take two to five days for big policy, procedural, or process changes, or 10 minutes for minor transitional changes. Allowing the camp to grow in prestige and reputation requires critical thought and connection; changing your plans on a whim will not get you there. Stay the course and, in time, regardless of the changes you may have to make during camp, both the operational and financial plans will pay off.

Third, the camp must hire and train high-quality staff that will help the camp achieve its mission and objectives. Consider candidates' experience working with children in various capacities as well as their educational levels or educational aspirations to work with children (i.e., becoming a teacher). Staff should be prescreened through background checks and provided high-quality training that teaches them how to use the tools, techniques, and other resources at their disposal to ensure high-quality programming for campers.

Fourth, the camp must make a commitment to campers and their families to provide good customer service and communication. This requires that you have excellent interpersonal skills and that you model the behavior for staff. Remember that parents can be challenging because of the vulnerability of the population you serve.

Fifth, keep sound judgment at the forefront of decision making, particularly regarding the safety of campers and counselors. Implement and follow the policies, procedures, and protocols that were established for the camp to manage risk. These policies should not be flexible, and procedures and protocols should be incorporated into staff training to provide clear instruction and guidelines. Sound judgment also includes making decisions that advance the mission and goals of the camp throughout the summer.

Sixth, to retain a flexible and charismatic staff, you need to be flexible—from the design of the camp itself to the breadth and depth of the staff training processes and the camp protocols. Develop staff members who understand the value of good customer service and troubleshooting and can engage campers and parents when things require flexibility. Develop flexible policies regarding camper, staff, and parent procedures, protocols, and processes. Additionally, have backup plans for inclement weather, for staff who are ill or experience emergencies, and for supplementary transportation when initial plans fall through.

Finally, you need to evaluate the staff, the programs, and the strategic plan on an annual basis. Include campers, staff, parents, and other colleagues in this process. Evaluations will help you develop and renew your program from year to year.

In addition to these suggestions, the strategic direction of the camp should incorporate the strategic plan and goals of the larger organization. The plan should address all of the services and programs that the organization provides, while being specific to the camp program. Because your ultimate goal is to brand your camp, if the larger organization already has a reputation, why not use it to move your camp forward?

SUMMARY OF ACTION STEPS

1. Develop a marketing strategy.
2. Implement plans.
3. Hire and train high-quality staff.
4. Commit to customer service and communication, whatever it takes.
5. Always employ sound judgment, with safety as the number one priority.
6. Be flexible.
7. Evaluate everything.

Figure 2.3 All camps should incorporate these general action steps; the details of these steps will vary from camp to camp based on the community served.

Conclusion

Creating or revitalizing a camp program begins with surveying the community, interpreting the survey data, and translating the data into programmatic decisions for the camp. Creating or selecting a survey instrument, distributing the survey, and interpreting the data can be accomplished in a number of ways. Regardless of whether data analysis is qualitative or quantitative, you should triangulate your findings to secure additional community or organizational support for your program. Resource inventories will help you make informed decisions regarding camp structure, resources, procedures, policies, and action steps for implementing a camp program.

Developing a high-quality summer camp program or revitalizing an existing one to supplement a larger organization's revenue is a difficult and lengthy process. Poorly planned camp programs lead to poorly implemented camp programs that do not progress the mission and goals of the organization. Chapter 3 discusses risk management, safety, and policy development.

Managing Risks

The number one concern in organized camping is safety. For this reason, you should discuss with your staff the many problems camps have faced regarding safety and risk management—from minor cuts and contusions to missing campers to camper death. The idea is not to scare your staff but rather to cement in their minds the concept that every decision must be made with campers' safety in mind. This is important, because employees can make very poor decisions in the name of fun or convenience that can unintentionally jeopardize the safety of the group.

A majority of parents do not expect camps or their staffs to be perfect, but they absolutely expect their children to be safe, both physically and emotionally. This chapter presents current laws and legislation regarding the standard of care camps are expected to maintain, health and safety standards current in today's world of organized camping, food preparation and distribution issues, and programming safety concerns. Staff recruitment, qualifications, and training are discussed in chapter 6, but keep in mind that a qualified staff with sound training is also a primary consideration in risk management and camper safety.

Laws and Legislation

Camp leaders exhibit the greatest amount of anxiety when issues of liability are discussed, planned, or considered. This is a good reason to learn the laws and legislation that rule the city or town, county, and state in which your camp operates. Keeping up with laws and legislation is not only good practice that legally protects the camp but also the right thing to do because it results in the creation of a caring community aimed at protecting vulnerable populations.

This section provides a general and minimal overview of the federal statute *in loco parentis* and highlights considerations for state and labor laws. It also addresses the importance of waivers to protect the camp program and the larger organization in a court of law. The section ends with a discussion of using the expertise and resources of the larger organization's risk management team, which many municipalities, colleges, and private clubs already have as part of their legal teams.

In Loco Parentis

The federal standard of care for caretakers of vulnerable populations in the United States is based on the notion of *in loco parentis* (Smith, 1991). *In loco parentis* literally means "in the place of the parent." It is a legal phrase that is used commonly in the field of education and casts a net of implications on school partners such as those found in after-school programs, retreats, field trips, day care, and community camp programs (Shivers, 1989). *In loco parentis* initially granted education providers and caregivers the authority to act as a parent when parents are not present. The scope and meaning of this has changed drastically over the last three decades. In the beginning, educators and legal analysts read the law very broadly and determined that caregivers had a great deal of flexibility in making decisions that affected children in the absence of their parents (Lefstein et al., 1982). This interpretation essentially protected caregivers who spanked, reprimanded, or paddled children.

Today, clear guidelines define the scope and authority of caregivers. Spanking, paddling, severe punishment, and any type of touching by untrained or uncertified staff are not protected in a court of law (Smith, 1991). Today's caregivers, including camp administrators, are expected to act in the best interest of the child by protecting them physically, emotionally, cognitively, and socially. This mandates that the organization's mission include a strong philosophy, fair goals, and reasonable objectives that focus on the development of the whole child. For most camps, this can be accommodated through the development of a solid discipline plan that is clear, consistent, and well communicated to campers, parents, and staff. Staff members should be trained well on verbal de-escalation techniques, understand the law as it applies to their counselor role, and receive ongoing training so that they can continue to improve these skills.

State and Labor Laws

In addition to understanding the federal legal implications of *in loco parentis,* camp personnel must also understand the standard of care mandated by state laws. Most states include all or some elements of *in loco parentis* in their laws governing education and children's services (Freeburg, 1949; Hulett, 1960; Lefstein et al., 1982). Because camp administrators are educators first, becoming familiar with those standards and what they mean for the camp is imperative in ensuring that staff are trained well and that policies and procedures are developed to protect the camper, the staff, and the organization.

Labor laws, both federal and state, govern many issues regarding how you relate to your staff. Generally speaking, day camp workers working six to eight hours are entitled to a 30-minute paid break every four hours (Ball & Ball, 1995). When hiring staff and planning schedules, be creative and try to adhere to staff members' requests for hours as much as possible. Additionally, it is always better to hire more staff members than you need rather than fewer because it provides much more flexibility in scheduling and meeting the criteria of the law. However, this is only feasible if you have factored additional staff costs into your overall budget, as discussed in chapter 2.

Waivers

Participation waivers have become a staple in just about every camp program. In this day of litigation, every program seems to want to ensure that the organization, and its actors, are clear of any wrongdoing or financial obligation in the event of camper injury.

Climbing can be a dangerous activity, so ensure that you have signed waivers from all participants and that supervisors are well trained, attentive, and decisive.

Waivers should be well written and use language that will hold up in court if the actions of the staff or program are ever questioned. A risk management or legal team should assist in constructing a waiver that is unique to the camp (Ball & Ball, 1995). If the camp program uses digital media and Internet marketing initiatives, the waiver should include permission to use a child's likeness (i.e., photo, video, or both) for these purposes. General waivers, or release of liability statements, and photo waivers should be part of registration forms. The CD-ROM includes sample waiver forms that can be used in registration materials:

- Form 3.1: Media and Photo Release for Minor Children
- Form 3.2: Field Trip Permission Slip
- Form 3.3: Kids Camp Application
- Form 3.4: Kids Camp Registration
- Form 3.5: Release of Liability

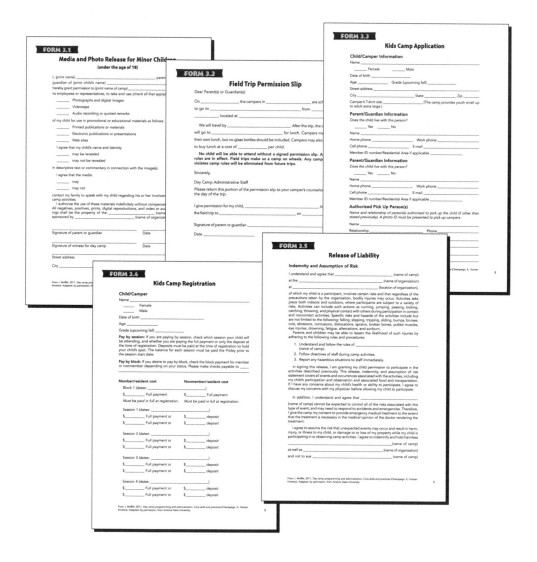

Participation waivers are a good practice, but it is important to remember that they will not hold up in court in cases in which staff or personnel demonstrated behavior lawfully deemed as negligent (Shivers, 1989). If staff members are not trained adequately, are not supervised to the reasonable standard of care mandated by law, or make extremely poor decisions, and a camper gets injured or dies, no waiver in the world will save the staff, the administration, or the program from liability. Waivers are not guarantees, and although they are necessary, it is far more important to invest time and resources in providing staff with the skills and resources they need to make sound decisions and to act quickly and appropriately in any given situation.

Risk Management Team

Municipalities, colleges, and private organizations most likely have protective structures established that help them identify risks. In many organizations, this is simply known as the risk management office, or the legal team. These professionals can help you identify potential risks, as well as determine the type and scope of language required on all camp documentation, such as the waiver.

Basic questions to ask when conversing with risk management teams include, but are not limited to, the following:

- What are the potential risks?
- How might these be managed?
- What constitutes negligence and gross negligence?
- How can this be minimized?
- What types of forms and documentation will be required?
- How will these documents be reviewed, stored, and completed?
- What will the follow-up procedures be?
- How will incidents be handled?
- How will federal, state, local, and organizational laws be incorporated into any documentation and language that help manage liability risk?
- Should the camp seek outside accreditation, and if so, why?

Including a parent or community member on the risk management team is a good way to solicit information from those whom the camp serves. This person can be an advocate for the camp by telling others about the level of thought, care, and concern the camp administrators put into making sure all children are safe at camp. This type of parent-to-parent advocacy goes a very long way in helping a new camp establish a patron base.

Health and Safety Standards

This section addresses medical history forms, infirmaries and health professionals, cleaning protocols, counselor-to-camper ratio, and food preparation and distribution. These are the most common health and safety concerns that camps must plan for.

Medical History Forms

Camper medical forms (also called health history forms) are necessary and often coupled with the release of liability, camp registration, and media waiver forms discussed previously (Northern Arizona University, 2001). Medical forms are intended to make sure that each camper has acquired the necessary preventive shots and boosters to minimize the spread of disease at camp. The most common incident at camps is illness due to the spread of viruses, bacteria, and disease (ACA, 2010c). Contact the state board of education to identify which immunizations are required for each grade or age of children attending school, and if applicable, transfer those requirements to the medical history form (see CD-ROM form 3.6: Health History). Children should not attend large group activities without the proper assurances that the risk of spreading disease has been minimized. Although medical history forms cannot guarantee against the spread of bacteria and germs in the camp program, they demonstrate a reasonable standard of care.

Medical history forms should list common allergies or any special needs campers may have. This information is reviewed by administrators, communicated to the counselors serving the child, and included in the camper's care plan. The care plan includes what to do should the camper be exposed to an allergen listed on the medical form. Counselors should be trained in handling emergencies when an allergic reaction strikes, as well as in minimizing exposure to allergens.

You also need to be concerned with the safety and well-being of your staff. Staff medical information cards are a quick, effective, and unobtrusive way to ascertain the needs of the staff (see CD-ROM form 3.7: Staff Medical Information). Staff medical information cards work in the same way as camper medical history forms, although they offer a bit more privacy because only camp administrators have access to staff medical forms. Information cards should minimally include emergency contact information, the name of the primary physician, allergies, special needs, or special instructions for care. Your risk management team may ask staff members to sign a waiver allowing the camp to provide care if necessary. This waiver does not mean that the organization will not have to provide workers' compensation, but it will allow the camp to access emergency and insurance information necessary for administering appropriate care.

FORM 3.7

Staff Medical Information

Name _____
Street address _____
City _____ State _____ Zip _____
Home phone (___) ___-____   Cell phone (___) ___-____
Insurance carrier _____ Policy number _____
Policyholder's name _____

Emergency Contacts

Name _____ Relationship to staff member _____
Phones: Daytime (___) ___-____   Cell phone (___) ___-____
Evening (___) ___-____
Name _____ Relationship to staff member _____
Phones: Daytime (___) ___-____   Cell phone (___) ___-____
Evening (___) ___-____

To the best of my knowledge, I am in good health and can participate as an actively engaged staff member at _____ (name of camp), with or without reasonable accommodation (note any accommodations below). I do not anticipate that I will have any health problems while participating in camp activities as part of my employment. However, _____ (name of camp) should be aware of the following medical conditions or medications that I take:

Accommodation(s) needed:
_____
_____
_____

Medications taken:
_____
_____
_____

From J. Moffit, 2011, *Day camp programming and administration: Core skills and practices* (Champaign, IL: Human Kinetics). Adapted, by permission, from University of Vermont Campus Recreation.

12

Infirmaries and Health Professionals

Overnight camps or larger day camps sometimes have an infirmary. Most infirmaries replicate school nurses' offices and are staffed by trained, certified, and experienced medical professionals. These personnel are responsible for distributing any type of medicine to campers requiring prescriptions or OTC (over-the-counter) medical aids. Additionally, these staff members are the experts in providing care when illness, injury, or other incidents happen (Ball & Ball, 1995). They are also responsible for documenting any camper incident, accident, or illness. Documentation of these occurrences must be practiced consistently among all staff, but health personnel provide an added cushion for ensuring that proper records are maintained.

If the camp can afford health professionals (this includes athletic trainers for college recreation departments and sport camps), it should have them on staff. Camps that cannot afford this type of staff should provide additional staff training to cover some of these areas.

If a child requires medication at camp and you do not have medical personnel, get a note from a parent or guardian allowing you to distribute the medication, as well as directions from the child's doctor describing how to do so (Ball & Ball, 1995). Any meds distributed at camp, whether prescription or OTC, should be logged and documented every single time (see CD-ROM form 3.8: Medicine Log). Obtain permission from a parent or guardian prior to distributing any OTC medication a child requests. This is good practice from a legal standpoint, but it also

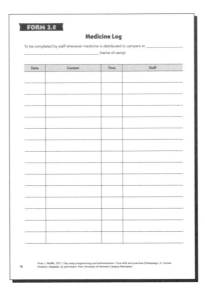

helps determine whether a child is allergic to anything in the medicine. A quick phone conversation with the child's parent or guardian can answer these questions, protect the child, and demonstrate the extent to which the camp ensures a child's safety.

Cleaning Protocols

Daily cleaning regimens are a simple way to reduce the spread of bacteria and germs. Encourage campers and staff to wash their hands regularly, and give each group the responsibility of cleaning up snack and lunch areas and throwing away trash. An alternative to hand washing that may be more convenient is to provide groups with hand sanitizers to apply quickly between activities. Creating a regular cleaning system with the custodial staff or camp staff is imperative. This should kill most bacteria and viruses, including methicillin-resistant Staphylococcus aureus (MRSA), a common bacteria that can cause severe health problems because of its resistance to common antibiotics.

In addition to lunch areas, group areas, and floors, equipment should also be cleaned regularly. This includes yoga mats, baseball bats and other striking equipment, and any type of weights. Finally, pinnies, bandanas, group T-shirts, or other fabrics used during camp should be washed daily with a detergent that kills viruses such as MRSA.

Counselor-to-Camper Ratio

The American Camping Association recommends a counselor-to-camper ratio not exceeding 1:15. For facility-based day camps, a ratio of 1:10 is recommended to reduce risk, increase supervision, and provide a high standard of care. The quality of instruction, time, patience, attention, and care that camp counselors can give in smaller groups far outweighs any monetary benefit from having a larger ratio. A smaller ratio allows counselors to care for campers on a physical, emotional, and social level, which is more difficult in large groups. Counselors may feel more comfortable, more confident, and more supported in smaller groups, which can translate into more meaningful interactions with campers. When this happens, campers believe that staff genuinely care about their well-being and are interested in them as individuals. Staff can tend to feel more stressed when they have to manage larger behaviorally challenging groups. Counselors, campers, and the programs themselves benefit from smaller ratios that focus on the needs of campers. The intergenerational relationships that form between counselors and campers when counselors feel supported rather than overwhelmed are another advantage of adhering to a smaller ratio in facility-based day camps. These relationships heighten the experience for campers and their parents and guardians and tend to advance the reputation of the camp, which invites long-term sustainability.

A ratio that is too small, however, can be just as problematic. Very small groups can present different, but equally frustrating, challenges to staff. Counselors often have difficulty motivating campers in very small groups because they lack the help of other campers to lead the group. Furthermore, because the camp program has to be fiscally responsible, very small groups are not an appropriate investment. Finding a ratio that works for the camp is the ultimate balancing act.

A small counselor-to-camper ratio (about 1:10) helps counselors feel more comfortable, confident, and supported while also letting them get to know their campers better.

Intergenerational Relationship Building

For two years, I worked at a camp for at-risk youth that was meeting fiscal and skill-development goals among campers but was struggling to help campers make good decisions regarding their behavior choices. Troubleshooting and conduct issues were mainstays for the counselors and administrative staff. Something had to change in our staff training protocol and in our philosophy in working with these children.

I began to wonder what would happen if we developed a plan to include intentional one-on-one time with each camper. What would this mean for the camp's schedule, the counselors' time, and the experience of the camper? Would it hurt our bottom line and further stress out my staff? Was the camp too large to make this manageable and effective? Would the intergenerational relationships that were formed help with the camp's behavior issues? I had very little data on the issue, because this was early in my career and I had not yet embraced the art of documentation and evaluation. I called other counselors for their opinions and asked my colleagues at the camp for feedback. What I gleaned from my impromptu conversations was that yes, the camp should try the idea, and that we should schedule time in the program to make sure it happened. Counselors also suggested that I hire one or two more staff per group to stagger schedules and reduce burnout, especially if I wanted each camper to spend five minutes a day with an adult role model.

I incorporated the suggestions into the new philosophy and redesigned staff training to include manageable ways for counselors to spend at least five minutes a day with all 30 of their campers. So as not to interrupt the flow of programs and developmental skills, I added longer transitional times, snack times, and lunch times to accommodate the one-on-one meetings. Many counselors were overwhelmed at first, but after I gave them concrete strategies for incorporating the meetings, rotating campers among them, and engaging campers in meaningful conversations, they became much more open to committing to the process.

In the first week, we struggled to balance these issues and reached only half of our campers each day. Nonetheless, discipline issues decreased. By the third week, staff had nailed the schedule and were managing their time effectively. Behavioral issues continued to decrease on a weekly basis, and counselors indicated that they felt more engaged with campers, less annoyed with their antics, and better suited to handle small disciplinary issues. I believe that these relationships allowed the staff to handle situations before they got out of control because campers respected the staff, felt genuinely cared for, and valued the connections with their counselors. Had I not committed to a 1:10 ratio during the camp day, my staff would have been less successful in holding intentional one-on-one time with each camper. Counselor-to-camper ratios are extremely important in intergenerational relationship building and should be planned for and adhered to as much as possible.

Food Preparation and Distribution

Food preparation and distribution may not be an issue at most facility-based camps housed in colleges, municipalities, or private organizations because food preparation facilities may not be available. For many facility-based camps, contracting with an outside food services entity is the closest they may come to food preparation and distribution. For these camps, following the guidelines of the food service organization is enough to cover the program from a liability standpoint. Most food service organizations already operate under state and federal laws imposed by governing authorities such as the U.S. Food and Drug Administration (FDA) or state health codes, among others.

Contracting food service organizations to provide lunch for campers is a convenient and relatively inexpensive way to provide an additional service. Colleges and universities may contract with the college's dining services to provide meals, whereas municipalities and private organizations may contract with local restaurants or business establishments to have food delivered to campers.

Some camp programs serve snacks only, so the rigid standards imposed by these governing agencies do not fully apply. However, camps providing this service should adhere to minimal food safety criteria. When organizing food preparation plans, consider the amount of time needed and how that time will affect the camp schedule. The following simple steps can help reduce the spread of food-borne illness in the camp:

1. Clean hands and food preparation surfaces often.
2. Separate foods during preparation to prevent cross-contamination.
3. Cook foods to the appropriate temperatures, and keep hot foods hot until they are eaten.
4. Chill foods quickly to safe temperatures, and keep cold foods cold until they are eaten.

According to the U.S. Centers for Disease Control (CDC, 2008), just one of these measures—clean hands—is the most important factor in preventing the spread of infectious diseases, including food-borne bacteria and illness.

Programming Safety Considerations

Programming safety considerations include common issues that all camps have to deal with on a daily basis and typically involve the work and judgment of the frontline staff—the counselors. Programming considerations include emergency action plans, certifications, first aid kits, communication tools, and structured games and activities.

Emergency Action Plans

An emergency action plan (EAP) is a necessary component of any camp program (Ball & Ball, 1995) and should be unique to the program. No standard EAP exists for facility-based camps, because facilities, communities, resources, and communication tools vary so greatly from camp to camp. However, not having a well-crafted, clear, action-oriented EAP is not acceptable. Furthermore, an EAP that is not communicated to staff; that is not visible to staff, campers, and parents and guardians; or that is used by poorly trained staff is as worthless as none at all. An effective EAP can make a difference in the outcome of any emergency. Dealing with an emergency effectively and quickly and following up with those involved in the emergency when appropriate demonstrate a standard of care that stresses safety.

In addition to an EAP for accidents and incidents that arise from the active day of a summer camp, you will need an EAP for gun threats, bomb threats, terrorist alerts, and missing persons, among other things. These EAPs must consider the full resources of the camp and describe an effective plan to put into action for any one of these incidents. It would be nice if we did not have to worry about such things. However, following the tragedies of Columbine, 9/11, and Virginia Tech, ignoring the possibility of such incidents would jeopardize the camp's commitment to providing a standard of care that ensures the safety of all staff and campers. The CD-ROM provides sample EAP forms for a number of emergencies:

- Form 3.9: Emergency Action Plan: Bomb Threats and Suspicious Packages
- Form 3.10: Emergency Action Plan: Severe Thunderstorm
- Form 3.11: Emergency Action Plan: Tornado Watch or Warning
- Form 3.12: Emergency Action Plan: Active Shooter
- Form 3.13: Emergency Action Plan: Missing Person
- Form 3.14: Emergency Action Plan: Aquatic Emergency

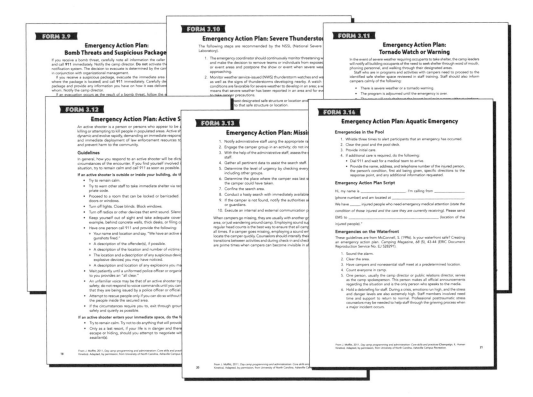

These samples are intended to help you create an EAP for any or all of these situations, but be sure to review them thoroughly and include any unique components of your camp program where appropriate. Risk management teams should be consulted when drafting an EAP.

Once you have developed the EAPs for your camp program, providing the necessary tools and skills to the entire staff (counselors, nurses, food preparers, volunteers, and so on) is the next step. Staff certifications, first aid supplies, communication tools, inclement weather procedures, and aquatic procedures are essential for providing care to campers and staff in emergency situations (Maurer-Starks, 2003) and will be discussed briefly in the following sections.

CAMP COUNSEL

General Action Steps for Medical Emergencies at Camp

- Step 1: Identify the emergency and clear the area of potentially unsafe particles or equipment.
- Step 2: Clear the area of bystanders to provide room to care for the camper, and assign a co-counselor to report the emergency on the radio using the identified code.
- Step 3: Do one of the following:
  - Give first aid treatment, wait for a camp leader to arrive, and complete an incident/accident report.
  - Call 911 and administer CPR. The area should be clear of all bystanders; only the first responder and a camp leader should provide care. Additional staff members should be notifying parents or guardians and waiting for medical personnel to direct them.
- Step 4: Continue caring for the camper until an EMT arrives, keeping the area clear.
- Step 5: Complete a detailed incident report and follow up with the camper and parents or guardians.

Certifications

CPR and first aid certification is a must for all camp staff members; staff certification not only ensures the implementation of the EAP but also sends a message to parents, guardians, and campers that the staff is prepared to handle emergencies (Sullivan & O'Brien, 2001). You should minimally require that your staff be certified in child first aid and CPR through the American Red Cross (ARC) or the American Heart Association (AHA) prior to the start of camp. You may choose to hire people who are already certified, or provide certification training during the staff training week. Either way, staff should be certified prior to any camper setting foot at camp.

Certification, however, does not guarantee that staff members will act appropriately in an emergency. Indeed, many certified people of all ages throughout many

Any swim instructors should carry the Water Safety Instructor (WSI) certification, as well as CPR and first aid certifications.

organizations do not act immediately or effectively when faced with emergencies. Like any skill, these need to be practiced, refreshed, and renewed to lessen the likelihood of inaction during an emergency (Maurer-Starks, 2003). To strengthen your staff's skills, offer a refresher course that includes scenarios and situations that are relevant to the camp. The course could take place during a weekly staff meeting or be offered one day a month as a paid program. Professionals from ARC and AHA could be on hand to test, refresh, and supervise the skill development of the staff.

Every staff member active in an aquatic program should also carry appropriate certifications and be provided ongoing training to refresh and sharpen their skills. If your camp offers swim lessons, the swim instructors should carry the Water Safety Instructor (WSI) certification. All of the lifeguards should be lifeguard certified, and all of the waterfront directors should be lifeguard certified, WSI certified, and swift water rescue certified; be trained in water boat safety; and carry any other certification necessary for administering a safe aquatic or waterfront program. (See CD-ROM form 3.15: Certifications Log.)

Finally, all staff members should be trained in and educated about blood-borne pathogens, and staff should know the safety precautions to take when dealing with bodily fluids. This is imperative for protecting not only other campers but also the staff. Most blood-borne pathogen training can be accommodated by an organization's risk management program, public safety office, or environmental safety protocol, so if the larger organization has these resources, it's best for facility-

FORM 3.15

Certifications Log

Counselor Certifications

based camps to tap into those professionals to train staff. If not, administrators will want to call local health departments and organize training for camp personnel. This includes the risk management divisions in colleges and universities, at private fitness clubs, in municipalities, and in parks and recreation departments.

A certification that may be useful to a camp serving at-risk youth or youth that are coping with very difficult life circumstances is the Crisis Prevention Intervention (CPI) certification. This training teaches appropriate strategies for de-escalating emotionally volatile children and for dealing with violent behavior. Counselors learn how to calm youth who are acting out emotionally through verbal communication, cues, and tools. They also learn how to quickly, respectfully, and painlessly restrain children when their behavior reaches a level at which verbal communication is no longer effective.

CPI certification provides legal protection in the same way that the CPR Good Samaritan law protects people who provide CPR in emergencies. If a staff member is CPI certified and has acted reasonably within the standard of care and within the scope of the CPI training, and restraint has been deemed necessary in protecting campers, that person will likely be protected in a court of law. CPI certification is not a "get out of jail free" card, however; it can have serious ramifications if a staff member uses it too soon, incorrectly, or inappropriately. CPI certification serves a purpose, but it may not be necessary for the goals and mission of every camp. Use great caution when determining whether CPI certification will be a staple of your staff certification requirements.

First Aid Kits

First aid supplies and kits are essential for implementing an EAP (Maurer-Starks, 2003). In addition to being well stocked and accessible to staff, first aid kits must also be used in the initial staff training and ongoing training sessions. Summer camp is a busy time, and it is easy to forget to check these items and make sure that enough supplies have been ordered. One way to make sure these kits are stocked is to have the closing shift employees check them before they leave each day. The counselors working at the end of the day should check their groups' first aid kits and restock them if necessary to prepare for the next day. If staff members discover that the overall supply is running low, a camp administrator with the authority to purchase more supplies should be notified immediately. The CD-ROM includes a list of items that every first aid kit at camp should include (see CD-ROM form 3.16: First Aid Kit Checklist).

Communication Tools

In addition to supplies and training, frontline camp workers also need a way to communicate with administrators or emergency personnel when required. Several types of two-way communication systems are available to ensure that staff members are able to contact camp leaders at any time. If the organization already uses radios as part of the daily operations, such as the sophisticated radio systems found on college campuses and in private fitness organizations, communication tools are already available. If your organization does not have the resources to attain this type of high-tech radio system, other options may be just as effective, provided you keep up with daily maintenance requirements.

Electronic stores and superstores typically carry two-way radio systems that range in price from $20 to $200. If you choose to use these less sophisticated two-way radios (or walkie-talkies), remember to factor in the cost of batteries, and always have replacement batteries for every radio on hand. You may want to include battery checks and replacements as part of the staff's opening or closing procedures. You cannot afford to have a group of campers and counselors head into their day without effective communication because of a shortage of batteries, or dead batteries. The benefits of these tools, especially in emergencies, far outweigh the cost (Maurer-Starks, 2003; Shivers, 1989).

Any communication tool employed to relay messages about camp happenings, emergencies, or incidents should use safety codes (also called radio codes) to describe the situation (Ball & Ball, 1995). Safety codes allow the counselor to tell the administrator what is happening without having to rehash the story over open airwaves. Safety codes lessen the likelihood of creating unnecessary panic in campers who overhear uncoded stories, and in their parents and guardians when campers eventually relay what they heard. Safety codes can avoid this type of incident while communicating the emergency quickly. Figure 3.1 presents radio codes that may be useful for any camp program in ensuring the safety and care of campers.

RADIO CODES

Code Orange	Minor injuries; first aid care required
Code Red	Serious or life-threatening accident or incident
Code Blue	Campers are fighting, hitting, or running away
Code Yellow	Missing camper (report and go to the office)
Code Gray	Inclement weather; follow directives; perform head counts
Code Brown	Vomit, fecal matter, or blood are in the pool; evacuate immediately; swim time is over; lifeguards and activity leader wait for the arrival of administrative staff

---

Figure 3.1 A sample of radio codes to employ in camps. Radio codes can be mounted on handheld radio sets for easy reference.

Although you may provide your staff with two-way communication tools, today's campers and counselors most likely also have access to personal cell phones. This form of communication should only be used when time is essential and the communication between staff and administrator is hindered. Alerting staff via the two-way radio is more effective than dialing members of the staff to get the word out that an emergency is happening. Making multiple phone calls slows down the response time of the staff and can inadvertently delay emergency medical response if medical attention is required. By using radio codes over the radio, every member of the staff hears that a situation has occurred and can respond accordingly while protecting the safety of their groups. Additionally, radio codes alert administrative staff immediately to the type of situation that is faced, and a call for medical attention can be made immediately, followed by a call to the parent or guardian. However, should a counselor use a cell phone to respond to an emergency situation, the action should not be frowned upon or discouraged. It is always better to be safe than sorry.

Campers with cell phones can create another set of issues. Campers may use cell phones to contact their parents or guardians without the staff's knowledge, take inappropriate pictures of other campers and staff without permission, text or e-mail inappropriately, or load images to the web that may violate cyber-bullying laws in some states. These activities do not fall under the heading of a healthy and active camp experience.

Depending on the size of your camp, two-way communication tools for every staff member may not be necessary. You need to decide which members require the tool and how that tool will be used from group to group, activity to activity, and day to day. For example, you may decide to give one staff member in a certain group, activity, or location a radio to communicate with administrators throughout the day. An example would be an archery instructor who works with every group throughout the day in an area in which accessible communication is needed. The important thing to keep in mind when setting up your communication systems is that contact with the administration should be able to be accomplished within seconds of an incident.

CAMP COUNSEL

Cell Phones at Camp

Cell phones have become a prime bullying tool. Children can be mean, and in today's technologically advanced world, they are finding more innovative and hurtful ways to bully, tease, and harm other children based on their personality traits, physical characteristics, or other superficial characteristics. The speed of modern technology allows children to bully other children so quickly that the counselor may not know what is going on until after the incident. For example, a child with a cell phone may take an unflattering picture of another child, get onto a social networking forum, and post the picture with a hurtful caption for everyone to view. Then the child sends the picture with the same caption to a group of people via texting. All of this can take place in less than three minutes. In this case, the camp has just allowed cyber bullying to happen and can be held liable.

As a provider of care, the camp is expected to provide a safe environment for everyone. For this reason, I recommend that cell phones be banned for campers. Campers wishing to call parents or guardians about any issue should be allowed and encouraged to use the camp phone in the administrative office. This can cut down opportunities for bullying and make camp administrators aware of campers' issues, especially those who are so unhappy that they want to call their parents and leave camp. Administrators are then in a position to stop the behavior that is happening in the group and to make sure that all campers feel validated, heard, helped, and cared for.

Staff-Facilitated Games

Staff-facilitated games and activities are an essential component of the day camp schedule, but they need to be fair, safe, fun, and age appropriate. Poorly planned games and activities can result in injury or lack of participation and cooperation on the part of campers. Train your counselors to address the following questions before initiating any activity with campers (Ball & Ball, 1995; Ditter, 2001).

- Are there any obstructions that may create unsafe conditions? Can these be solved quickly and reasonably? If not, do not play the game.

- Do the current rules need to be modified to provide a safer environment or a friendlier noncompetitive activity?
- What is the worst thing that could happen if this game is played? Is that manageable, or do the risks outweigh the benefits? If so, do not play the game.
- Do the campers understand the rules? Can they repeat them?
- How will you reinforce good sporting behavior? Offer shouts of encouragement during the game and boisterous praise afterward.
- Are campers exhibiting unsafe behavior? Don't be afraid to call the game off if campers are not cooperating and things are getting out of hand.

Staff-facilitated games and activities need to be fair, safe, fun, and age appropriate.

Camp counselors often ask campers what they would like to do. Although encouraging campers to be involved in the camp experience is important, it is more important to recognize when a "fun" idea is a potentially dangerous idea. Too many times, counselors wanting to make sure that campers are having fun or that they are befriending campers quickly forget the previous checklist and allow kids to play games that are unsafe. Counselors who are eager to please campers and have fun with them, or who just have difficulty saying no, can create a host of physical problems for the campers and legal problems for the camp (Taylor, 2001). Make sure you explain this issue clearly to all staff during training week. Remember, situations that can seem innocent or sublime can quickly turn into a lawsuit waiting to happen.

A prime example of this occurred one summer day in the Midwest when a counselor was clearly tired and unimaginative. She asked campers what they wanted to do, and they decided to tie other campers around the neck with a rope, have them sit on a scooter, and pull them around the gym floor. Indeed, the campers had a ball, but the counselor and the administrators who immediately stopped the game were horrified to see that the rope had created a rope burn around one camper's neck. Not only was this not a safe game, but it could have been argued that the camper had been abused. Although that argument may not have proven fruitful, the camp most certainly could have been found guilty of poor judgment and possibly neglect.

The only option at that point for camp administrators was damage control, which came in the following ways:

- A phone call to the child's guardian
- Admittance of a mistake and reassurance that a protocol was in place to end such decisions
- Education and training of the staff member (some camps may have chosen to terminate the staff member)
- A verbal apology by the counselor to the child and the child's guardian
- Camp administrators admitting their own culpability and understanding that the camp may have lost that family as a member of the community

Although this example may seem extreme and unrealistic, similar incidents of poor judgment and lack of caution can create similar consequences for the camp. Even everyday activities that are not properly monitored and controlled by the staff can create a domino effect. Consider an activity that requires the use of an instrument to strike at a moving object. Campers who are naturally excited by such a game may become overzealous and stand too close to other campers using the instrument. In such cases, it is only a matter of time before an overzealous camper is hit, and the other campers may not be convinced that the hit was "on accident." Forward-thinking staff members who explain rules clearly, take safety precautions, and are actively monitoring the activity can prevent such incidents.

More specific information, tips, strategies, and suggestions for training staff on designing innovative games are discussed in chapter 6, Staffing the Camp. Additionally, developing positive group dynamics, adjusting to various learning styles, leadership, conflict resolution, transitional periods, and dealing with bullying are discussed in that chapter.

Conclusion

Ensuring the safety of campers and staff must be at the forefront of all decisions. Following state and federal laws for providing a reasonable standard of care on a consistent basis is a minimum expectation for creating a safe camp. Going beyond these standards to create a safe and healthy environment for both campers and staff creates a community with a reputation for caring.

Camp stewardship involves being familiar with state and federal laws and working with risk management and legal teams to develop necessary structures that protect campers, staff members, and the program. Through the development of legal waivers, medical history forms, sound policies, and a qualified staff, camp programs can be proactive in protecting campers throughout the camp season. Camps with a reputation for being fun, safe, and caring experience growing enrollment as a result of parent advocacy in the larger community.

Developing Camp Policies

Camp policies are crucial to a facility-based camp program because they provide rules, guidelines, and boundaries for everyone involved. Policies are needed for parents and guardians, campers, counselors, and the organization so that the most mundane and routine processes, such as registration and fee schedules, can be carried out swiftly and fairly. Likewise, well-thought-out and consistently implemented policies level the playing field for all campers, counselors, parents, and guardians because they outline what to expect. Camp policies also help camp administrators respond to occurrences at camp.

This chapter addresses policies for registration and refunds, camper drop-off and pickup, discipline, and parental communication. The chapter concludes with a brief look at other policies for issues such as inclement weather, medicine distribution, homesickness, and attire.

Registration and Refunds

Camp registration and refund policies should be sensitive to the needs of families, while also protecting the camp. Strong policies clearly spell out what instances result in refunds and how, when, and where patrons can register. A good policy now saves an incredible amount of work later.

Registration and refund policies should be communicated clearly and often. They should be specific but flexible to allow the camp director to make exceptions based on patrons' situations. Sometimes the camp director may decide not to grant an exception to the policy. This sends a message to patrons that the administration is open to hearing about situations that may need accommodation but that the needs of the camp must sometimes come before those of individuals. Families see firsthand that the camp leadership is not rigid but does have boundaries. For many families, that is more than enough to keep them registering session after session, even if they sometimes don't get exactly what they want.

Questions to Answer When Developing a Registration Policy

- Who can register?
- When can they register?
- How and where will they register?
- What happens if they register after the deadline?
- What happens if a child falls on the cusp of an age group? How will the camp determine which group (older or younger) to put the child in?
- What happens when a child wants to withdraw from a session?
- What happens when a child wants to switch sessions?
- Can children request to be in certain groups?
- Will the families be required to pay at registration? What amount? How will payment be accepted? What will happen if payment is late? (See CD-ROM form 4.1: Late Fee Notice.)
- Will families be required to complete a medical history form for each camper during registration? If so, how will this sensitive material be collected (e.g., online form, registration form, short history)?
- What happens to photos of children taken at camp? (For more details, see Camp Counsel on p. 67.)

Questions to Answer When Developing a Refund Policy

- How does the camp's financial operation work in line with the larger organizational protocol?
- How can the policy protect the camp from nonpayers or last-minute dropouts?

- How can the policy allow for flexibility for families without taxing the camp staff?
- Is the policy clearly written?
- How will the policy be communicated?
- How much money will a family receive back for early or late withdrawal?
- Will an administrative fee be assessed for all refunds?
- What circumstances of late notice will result in a refund? What will not?
- How will the refund be paid? Will this change if the family is on a payment plan?
- Who has the final say regarding refund policies for the camp?

Every organization has unique considerations, but most will want to answer the preceding questions to create a substantial registration and refund policy.

Some camps may need to consider scholarships, lunch options, tax identification issues for child care, and cost breakdowns in their registration and refund policies. A cost analysis allows families to see what they are paying for and understand the financial implications of sending children to a camp that provides exceptional care and promotes physical activity.

CAMP COUNSEL

Photos Taken at Camp

Many camp liability waivers ask parents and guardians to grant permission to take and use pictures of their children. During registration, parents and guardians may ask you what will happen to the pictures. Be prepared to tell them whether pictures will be used in future marketing and registration materials, and how you will communicate this to them. When developing language around picture permission, include a statement indicating what will happen to the pictures; parents and guardians have a right to know that pictures of their children could show up in public marketing campaigns, including on the Internet. Letting them know this up front will increase their comfort level.

Scholarships

Although facility-based day camps tend to be quite affordable, some families cannot afford them. Registration policies can also include camp scholarship information, requirements, and application forms.

Questions to Answer When Developing a Scholarship Policy

- Will there be a separate scholarship application (see CD-ROM form 4.2: Scholarship Application), or will the information be included on the basic registration form?
- How many scholarships will the camp extend?
- How will scholarship campers be subsidized?

- What financial requirements will qualify children for scholarships?
- How will the scholarship application be received and analyzed?
- Who will determine which applicants receive scholarships?

Offering scholarships allows the camp to reach children who would not otherwise have the opportunity to experience camp. Additionally, it promotes the benefits of organized camping and makes programs and services available to a new audience that may become supporters and advocates for the camp program and the organization. Scholarships also advance the camp's reputation, which further ensures the long-term sustainability of the program.

Lunch Options

Offering lunch to campers can be a headache, especially if lunch service and storage facilities are limited. However, an optional lunch program can pay off in terms of both service and revenue. Many parents may decide that the convenience of not having to pack a lunch every day is worth the cost of the service. The CD-ROM includes forms for organizing camper lunch and snack requests (see CD-ROM form 4.3: Lunch Order and form 4.4: Snack Order). A program like this will require policies for registration, payment, and refunds.

College-based camps can partner with campus dining services to offer lunch to campers. This service may be boxed cold lunches delivered to the camp, or it may be a sit-down meal. However the lunch is negotiated, it's important that the camp not tax the dining staff or service. If a camper lunch service begins to feel like too much work, or too many things are going wrong, it may require some adjustments.

Contracting out to a registered food service provider is an easy, affordable, and legal way to provide lunch or snacks to campers. The service must also meet a financial goal—either realizing a profit or simply covering the cost of the program. If the program is easy and efficient and provides healthy and tasty food to campers, families using it may encourage others to register. The bottom line is

FORM 4.3

Lunch Order

To order lunch for your child, please complete this form and provide payment at the time of camp registration. Lunch orders must be paid in full one week before the start of the camp session.

Camper name _____

Group _____ Session_____

Cold lunch option ($_____/day)

All cold lunches include the following:
- Choice of six-inch sub (either turkey or ham)
- Piece of fruit (no choice of fruit available)
- Chips (Lays potato chips)
- Cookie (no choice of cookie available)
- Drink (juice or milk)

Please select a sub for each day and let us know if you want no cheese on the sub.

Monday:	❑ Turkey	❑ Ham	❑ No cheese
Tuesday:	❑ Turkey	❑ Ham	❑ No cheese
Wednesday:	❑ Turkey	❑ Ham	❑ No cheese
Thursday:	❑ Turkey	❑ Ham	❑ No cheese
Friday:	❑ Turkey	❑ Ham	❑ No cheese

All sandwiches come with mayonnaise and mustard packets and lettuce and tomato.

Hot lunch options are $_____ per day, and there are no choices available with this option. Campers must eat what is served by the food provider.

❑ Monday   ❑ Tuesday   ❑ Wednesday   ❑ Thursday   ❑ Friday

Total cost of lunches: $_____

Method of payment: Cash _____   Check (Check #: _____)

From J. Moffitt, 2011, *Day camp programming and administration: Core skills and practices* (Champaign, IL: Human Kinetics).

3

FORM 4.4

Snack Order

To order a snack for your child, please complete this form and provide payment at the time of camp registration. Snack orders include two snacks per day and must be paid in full one week before the start of the camp session.

Camper name _____

Group _____ Session_____

Snack option ($_____/day)

Weekly Snack Menu

Typically, campers are provided with fruit and juice in the morning and a variety of snacks and fruit drinks in the afternoon.

Monday

Morning snack _____ Drink _____

Afternoon snack _____ Drink _____

Tuesday

Morning snack _____ Drink _____

Afternoon snack _____ Drink _____

Wednesday

Morning snack _____ Drink _____

Afternoon snack _____ Drink _____

Thursday

Morning snack _____ Drink _____

Afternoon snack _____ Drink _____

Friday

Morning snack _____ Drink _____

Afternoon snack _____ Drink _____

Total cost of snacks: $_____

Method of payment: Cash _____   Check (Check #: _____)

From J. Moffitt, 2011, *Day camp programming and administration: Core skills and practices* (Champaign, IL: Human Kinetics).

4

that solid, value-added services increase the overall view of the camp and help build its reputation.

If your camp does not have the option of an in-house food service provider, you may decide not to offer lunch. In this case, you will need to determine whether the food storage space is adequate for keeping bagged lunches cool until lunchtime. If so, collect children's lunches at the beginning of the day and refrigerate them until lunchtime. Obviously, you will need a system for this process, but this is

For camp programs without appropriate storage and refrigeration, instructing parents to pack brown bag lunches that will keep until lunchtime is an effective way to cut costs at camp and manage lunchtime processes without affecting the camper experience.

relatively easily created and can be managed by counselors. If no such storage exists, notify parents and guardians so that they can prepare lunches for their children that do not require refrigeration.

Tax Identification

Most recreational day camps have tax identification numbers associated with the business and operations of child care. This number is very important to parents and guardians, especially from January to April every year. Be sure to post the tax identification number in several places that are accessible to parents and guardians, and communicate those locations. Otherwise, you can expect to field phone calls from parents and guardians asking for the number for tax purposes during the first few months of every year.

Cost Breakdowns

If your camp is more affordable than other area camps, it may be good marketing to provide an estimated breakdown of the cost of camp in terms of trips, food, equipment, and other factors. This allows families to see what they are paying for and identify operating costs they may not have thought about. However, be careful when breaking down costs, and avoid using actual dollar amounts. These may invite questions about the expenses, and you may end up getting unsolicited advice that is rarely helpful. More often than not, opening the financial specifics to the camp constituency invites headaches. Parents and guardians do not need to know the cost of each item; they just need to see that they are paying for a great deal of engagement that benefits their children.

One way to achieve this is to do a market analysis of camps in your area (see table 4.1). While not revealing the exact cost of items, you demonstrate that your camp is offering either a lower-cost or a higher-quality program.

Table 4.1 Market Analysis of Area Camps

	Program areas	Services	Facilities used	Cost
Camp 1	5	Lunch, after care	3	$175/week
Camp 2	7	Lunch, snack	5	$195/week
Camp 3	4	Sibling discounts	3	$165/week
Our camp	6	Lunch, snack, after care, sibling discounts	7	$185/week

Drop-Off and Pickup

Transferring the responsibility of campers from parents and guardians to the camp and back can be stressful. During drop-off and pickup, children's safety must never be jeopardized. Policies and procedures surrounding these events are extremely important because poor management practices can lead quickly to mistakes for which the camp may be viewed as liable.

Having drop-off and pickup policies and procedures in place can help ensure the safety of campers.

Staff members must arrive early enough in the day to prepare for receiving children as well as to plan for the camp day. Depending on the financial situation of the camp and the size of the staff, this may require innovative scheduling. Staggering counselor schedules and providing administrative oversight may be the best way to balance the camp's financial needs and campers' safety needs. With staggered schedules, counselors will not have to work long hours beyond what the camp has budgeted, and at least one administrator can be present at all times.

You will also need to document the transfer of the child from parent or guardian to camp and back at both check-in and checkout. A sign-in and sign-out sheet (see CD-ROM form 4.5: Camper Check-In and Checkout) is a simple way to manage this. You need to decide whether you will allow children to check themselves in or require parents or guardians to formally check their children in. Parent and guardian check-ins are more legally sound and give the staff the chance to connect with parents and guardians at the beginning of the day. This helps the staff at checkout by familiarizing them with families. Most important, parent and guardian signatures demonstrate the transfer of campers to the camp and back again at each function. Camper signatures demonstrate the attendance of the camper but are less legally sound because they do not indicate that the legal guardian was aware of the transfer. Depending on the camp, this may or may not be an issue, but it is always better to err on the side of caution, making adult signatures the preferred method of transferring campers.

The registration form should include a list of people allowed to pick up the child from camp. Any person not listed on the parent or guardian approval section should

FORM 4.5

Camper Check-In and Checkout

Parents and guardians must initial in the In and Out columns each day to verify that the child has been checked in or out.

Name	Group	Counselor initials	MONDAY		TUESDAY		WEDNESDAY		THURSDAY		FRIDAY	
			In	Out	In	Out	In	Out	In	Out	In	Out
1.												
2.												
3.												
4.												
5.												
6.												
7.												
8.												
9.												
10.												
11.												
12.												
13.												
14.												
15.												
16.												
17.												
18.												
19.												
20.												

Notes

Staff may indicate here who has EpiPens, late/early arrivals, etc.

_____
_____
_____
_____
_____
_____

From J. Moffitt, 2011, Day camp programming and administration: Core skills and practices (Champaign, IL: Human Kinetics). Adapted, by permission, from University of Vermont Campus Recreation.

not be allowed to check out a camper without written consent from a parent or guardian. Consider developing a form that parents and guardians can complete to give someone not listed on the registration form permission to check their children out (see CD-ROM form 4.6: Third Party Pickup Request). This provides documentation for the camp should any question arise about who picked a child up, and it reminds families that the safety of campers is paramount to the camp. The policy regarding permission to check campers out should be enforced consistently, regardless of any personal relationships the staff may have with parents or others.

Consider a policy that requires notification of early departures and late arrivals (see CD-ROM form 4.7: Early Departure Request and form 4.8: Late Arrival Notification). Included should be a policy requiring all visitors to sign in at the camp headquarters before entering the camp (see CD-ROM form 4.9: Visitor Sign-In Log).

FORM 4.6

Third Party Pickup Request

I, _____ (parent or guardian), am

requesting that my child, _____ (camper),

in the _____ (group name) group, be picked up by

_____ (name of third party).

I understand that third party pickups require appropriate identification to verify the individual picking up my child. I have communicated this requirement to the person listed above, who will have appropriate identification when picking up my child. _____ (parent or guardian initials)

Will the camper be picked up during checkout by this person? Yes ____ No ____

If no, what time will this person be picking up the camper? _____

If no, where have you instructed this person to pick up the camper? _____

_____   _____
(Parent or guardian signature)   (Date)

From J. Moffitt, 2011, Day camp programming and administration: Core skills and practices (Champaign, IL: Human Kinetics).

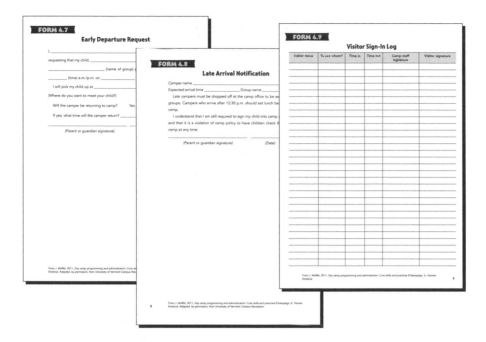

From J. Moffit, 2011, *Day camp programming and administration: Core skills and practices* (Champaign, IL: Human Kinetics). Adapted, by permission, from University of Vermont Campus Recreation.

Families need to know where they can park when dropping off and picking up their children. If your host organization has strict parking rules that are enforced by security (e.g., colleges and business fitness facilities), obtain an agreement that exempts the camp and families from any parking fines during drop-off and pickup times. Parents and guardians not picking up or dropping off campers during those times, or who arrive at another time of day, should be subject to ticketing rules, and the camp should not be responsible for any tickets they receive.

Accommodating families while adhering to the organizations' protocols is essential for the success of both entities. Your camp may need parking lot traffic to flow differently during the summer or security personnel to maintain safety during high-traffic times of day. Communicate your needs in advance to security personnel, and keep the goals of the security team in mind when negotiating parking terms and protocols.

For the added protection of families that have indicated people who may not pick up campers (this is often seen in foster families or families in custody battles), consider implementing a policy that requires adults to show proper identification to check out their children. Although this may seem an added, and perhaps unnecessary, burden on parents and guardians, the benefit of ensuring campers' proper departures far outweighs this inconvenience. A camp that does not consistently enforce and regulate these procedures and policies opens itself to a detrimental level of risk that could result in severe consequences.

Developing systems to manage and enforce drop-off and pickup policies demands forethought. Although these procedures will vary greatly from camp to camp, the questions regarding liability and negligence should be the guiding factors in implementation. In addition, staff members should understand what is expected of them at these times and be trained to handle any questions or conflicts that may arise. A member of the administration should always be available to help with questions or conflicts during these times.

Discipline

In this age of litigation, you must put extra care into determining discipline policies and procedures for both counselors and campers. In an ideal world, campers would come to camp and be thoughtful, cheerful, and respectful, and enjoy the experience of just being a kid at camp. However, campers and counselors come to camp with varying expectations, backgrounds, behaviors, and attitudes. Your task is to ensure the greater good while providing opportunities for campers and counselors to improve.

This section is not intended to be a comprehensive discussion of discipline at camp, because camps experience a variety of behavior issues based on their mission, geography, and clientele. Conduct a thorough study of the needs of your constituents before enforcing any of the policies recommended in this section.

Policies for Campers

Before creating any discipline policies, you need to articulate your philosophy on disciplining children. Once you have done that, take extra care to implement procedures that are consistent with your philosophy. Figure 4.1 provides a suggested step-by-step guide to developing and implementing camper discipline protocols at facility-based camps. Additionally, you should use forms to document camper behavior and the camp's response to that behavior. The CD-ROM offers several forms for practitioner use regarding camper behavior. See form 4.10: Camper Incident Log, form 4.11: Camper Incident Report, form 4.12: Behavior Contract, and form 4.13: Behavior Guidance Agreement.

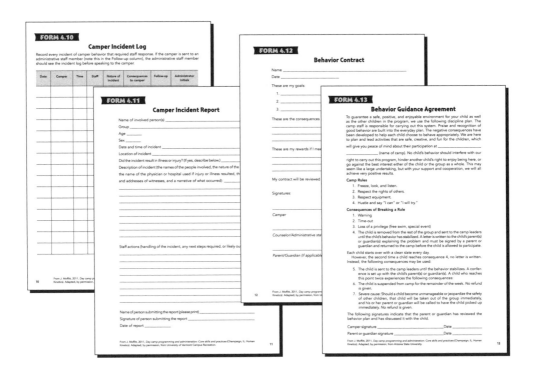

DEVELOPING CAMPER DISCIPLINE PROTOCOLS

1. Call the local schools and ask about the discipline plans enforced in the school system
   a. Educational philosophies of accountability and behavior modification in the geographical area of the camp are often the best philosophies to adopt because they tend to be in line with state and federal expectations, are safe for campers and the camp, and may be familiar to those attending.
   b. Familiarity with the discipline plan at camp invites greater adherence to the policy by parents, guardians, and campers.
   c. Communicate the philosophy and the plan to parents and guardians early, clearly, and consistently.
   d. Ask parents and guardians to review the behavior expectations, discipline plans, and potential consequences with their children prior to coming to camp.

2. Determine whether this philosophy and the associated discipline plans can be easily and consistently enforced at the camp.
   a. Decide what modifications and resources will be required to implement this discipline policy at camp.
   b. Plan how each incident will be documented to protect the actions of the camp and educate parents or guardians and the camper regarding the behavior.

3. Determine when and how incidents will be communicated to parents and guardians.
   a. Decide what incidents and repetitive behavior will require a call to parents or guardians.
   b. Develop a behavior modification protocol that will be discussed with the camper and parents or guardians, when necessary, to help the child make better choices at camp and ultimately modify behavior to ensure successful participation at camp.

4. Determine what level of training will be required to prepare the staff for enforcement and implementation.
   a. Start with an explanation of the philosophy and how it ties in to the mission of the camp.
   b. Outline the discipline plan that is associated with the philosophy and communicate the staff role in the implementation of the plan.
   c. Provide tools and resources to the staff so that they are not afraid to ask for help and develop their group management skills based on the age groups that they will be working with.
   d. Give examples and demonstrate appropriate and inappropriate ways to handle several discipline situations that may arise at camp.

Figure 4.1   Steps to developing a camper discipline philosophy.

Policies for Counselors

Counselor discipline will be informed by several factors, including institutional or organizational protocols regarding staff infractions and performance improvement plans. Develop policies and procedures that are in line with the organization's expectations and that are clear and consistent with the standards of day care providers as mandated by state and federal statutes. Like camper discipline, counselor discipline should be documented (see CD-ROM form 4.14: Counselor Discipline Log). Figure 4.2 includes the minimal considerations of such a policy, which are not intended to be all inclusive.

Like all policies, counselor discipline policies should be updated annually and clearly communicated to everyone involved. However, communicating staff discipline protocols to families may not be necessary, nor is it professional. A general reassurance to parents and guardians that systems are in place for holding staff accountable when mistakes are made is sufficient. In fact, the only time it may be necessary to communicate counselor discipline procedures to parents and guardians is when an incident occurs and the staff member must be defended or terminated (based on the incident).

Parental Communication

Communicating with parents and guardians can be time consuming and challenging depending on the size and clientele of the camp. Despite these obstacles, determining the most appropriate way to communicate with them, as well as how frequently, is a worthwhile investment of time and energy. Your biggest dilemma is in striking a balance between keeping parents and guardians informed and overloading them with information. Parents and guardians, like children, have a

DEVELOPING COUNSELOR DISCIPLINE PROTOCOLS

1. The policy must be in line with the organization's philosophy of employee relations.
   a. Consider the staff accountability policy of the larger organization and develop a similar policy for camp staff accountability.
   b. Connect the role of camp staff to the larger organization to demonstrate that the camp is part of the larger team, vision, and mission for serving the community.
2. The policy should include specific instances that are relevant to camp.
   a. Larger organization accountability policies may include examples of what happens to staff when they do not fulfill specific expectations of the job, but those for a camp program may look different.
   b. For example, camp staff misbehavior will include being late to work, dressing outside the scope of the uniform, yelling at campers, and inappropriately disciplining campers. The latter two will look very different at a camp dealing with minors than in the larger organization, and these actions require severe action by the camp.
3. The policy should be fair and clearly communicated.
   a. The policy should be written using clear language and good grammar.
   b. The policy should be reviewed at staff trainings and made available throughout the camp.
4. The policy should offer counselors opportunities to correct their mistakes and grow.
   a. Implementing a work performance improvement plan is good practice for infractions caused by behavior that can be improved.
   b. The work performance plan should encourage counselors to think critically about how to improve and their level of responsibility so that they can grow professionally.
5. The policy should be consistently enforced.
   a. Camp administrators must not play favorites based on personalities.
   b. All infractions, regardless of who committed them, should be handled consistently.
6. The policy should be flexible enough to include a variety of situations and behaviors.
   a. Insubordination should always be approached as a learning moment.
   b. Gross misrepresentation of the camp through inappropriate or illegal behavior should always result in termination.
7. The policy should include sexual harassment guidelines of the organization and city, state, or federal government.
   a. Larger organizations should already have a staff harassment policy.
   b. The camp may need to include an amendment to the policy for when staff feel they are being harassed by campers, which is likely in camps that serve older children.

Figure 4.2 Counselor discipline considerations when developing a policy regarding staff accountability.

wide variety of expectations of camp; some want to be flooded with information, others want no information, and still others may view too much information as an inability to manage children's programs and provide care.

A flexible parental communication policy can help you make your camp's intentions known to all families. No universal policy is adopted by all camps, because each camp serves a unique population. Nevertheless, the minimal considerations listed in figure 4.3 may help you create a sound policy.

Creating a parental communication policy is worthwhile because it creates an open, honest, and consistent communication pattern between the camp and parents and guardians, which ultimately builds strong relationships. It also saves you a great deal of time in the long run. This is especially true when you use sound procedures and tools to carry out the policy on a consistent basis. Like campers, parents and guardians want to know what to expect from the camp; giving them this information up front will save you from having to discuss or explain issues individually, or apologize for the lack of communication. A communication policy clearly outlines the goals of camp administration in communicating issues to parents and guardians and reinforces the camp's commitment to serving children and their families.

Other Policy Considerations

The day-to-day implementation of camp schedules and camper care results in other concerns and occurrences. Following are examples of simple, flexible, and effective policies related to four common issues at facility-based day camps.

The following four policies are adapted, by permission, from University of Vermont Campus Recreation.

Inclement Weather

During the summer there may be days when inclement weather does not allow us to participate in planned camp activities outdoors. The camp has identified the [location] and [location] as indoor locations that will allow us to facilitate camp activities. On rainy days, [names of indoor activities, if applicable] activities should not be affected. The pool will close during inclement weather, and counselors will identify an indoor activity to engage campers in during their normally scheduled swim time. Due to the pool schedule for all individuals using the facility, swim time will not be rescheduled on inclement weather days.

Homesickness and Illness

If a camper is experiencing homesickness at camp, our staff will employ several strategies to help the camper acclimate to camp without parental influence. Strategies include discussions with campers outlining specific items that are missed, drawing pictures of said items, discussing strategies the child can use to have fun at camp when homesickness is on their mind, highlighting the benefits of camp, and comparing the activities they are engaged in to those that they would be doing at home. Finally, if all of these strategies fail, the child will be permitted to call parents or guardians.

DEVELOPING A PARENTAL COMMUNICATION POLICY

1. Make it clear what instances require the camp to communicate with parents or guardians daily and how the camp will initiate communication.
   a. Campers are injured: phone call
   b. Campers forget their lunch: phone call
   c. Campers are ill: phone call
   d. Camp had to cancel a field trip: e-mail
   e. Facility emergencies: e-mail followed by individual phone calls
   f. Fighting or extreme behavioral issues: phone call to arrange a face-to-face meeting
   g. Minor behavior issues for which the camp seeks support and reinforcement of discussed issues at home: face-to-face conversation at the end of the day
   h. Extremely good behavior: face-to-face conversation at the end of the day
2. Make it clear how the camp will communicate throughout the camp season (i.e., what strategies will be employed from registration to evaluation).
   a. Develop a parent manual that can be downloaded online.
      i. The manual should include all policies.
      ii. The manual should include all procedures and plans.
      iii. The manual should include all contact information.
      iv. The manual should include the camp mission and goals.
      v. The manual should be easily accessible and compatible with varying computers and software programs.
   b. Send payment reminders by e-mail.
      i. This is useful for registration purposes.
      ii. Keep in mind that late payments should always be communicated over the phone.
      iii. Field trip notifications should occur at the beginning of the week.
   c. Electronic updates (e-mail, e-newsletter, links to web sites, and so on)
      i. Schedule changes
      ii. Minor cuts or scrapes the camper got at camp can be handled via e-mail.
      iii. Major injuries and incidents should always be handled by phone.
   d. Electronic weekly camp newsletters
      i. Let parents and guardians know what happens at camp with brief descriptions and pictures.
      ii. If available, this informs parents and guardians about what their child was up to all week while reinforcing that the camp provides outstanding programming and care for all campers.
3. Make it clear how parents and guardians can communicate with the camp.
   a. Give parents and guardians the camp office phone number, and make sure someone is always available to answer it so that they know they can reach the camp and their children whenever needed.
   b. Provide a camp e-mail address for parents and guardians who prefer electronic communication.
   c. If cell phones are banned for campers, make sure parents and guardians can reach the camp at any time.

Figure 4.3 Suggested steps in creating a parental communication policy at camp.

Using E-Newsletters to Educate Parents

I have received many inquiries from parents about special needs, home-sickness, and other issues they were concerned about with regard to their children. While I am always sensitive to the concerns of parents, the number of inquiries and special requests at a large camp can become daunting and extremely difficult to keep up with during a busy camp season. I decided that one way to mitigate these issues was to develop and send e-newsletters to parents once a week. The point of the e-newsletters was to educate parents in preparation for the upcoming week about camp needs, programs, schedules, parking reminders, and a contact for special needs coordination. I called this e-newsletter "Welcome to Camp" because it was sent one week before the start of camp and included all of the aforementioned items plus camp contact information and weekly field trip schedules. Once I started that, the number of phone calls and questions I received from parents dropped substantially, and we were able to focus on coordinating the special needs of campers that required accommodation.

In addition to the "Welcome to Camp" e-newsletter, I also began developing and sending another e-newsletter that highlighted the camp activities for the week. This correspondence included photos, schedules, activity listings, camper quotes of the week, and information on every age group that was served. This was used as a way to show parents what their children had been engaged in all week long. I called it "Camp Wrap" and sent it to parents via e-mail on the last day of the week. The weekly wrap-up was a way for parents to stay abreast of what was happening at camp without having to seek out correspondence from me or counselors regarding program scheduling and activities. This allowed me and my staff to focus on providing information to parents regarding their children's behavior or any accidents or incidents that needed to be communicated to parents.

Determining the design and information to include in an e-newsletter depends on the type of camp, the communication policy, and the procedures the camp requires when preparing campers and their families. It will also depend on whether camps implement a photo release and waiver. I highly recommend including something like an e-newsletter in the communication policy of camps for the following reasons:

- Increased relationships with families come in handy when problems occur.
- You have the ability to set rules about which incidents require instant parent or guardian notification (illness, fighting, injury) and which do not (schedule changes).
- Using online tools, such as e-mail, e-newsletters, and web sites, makes communication easy and affordable, adding value to the social and economic sustainability of the camp program.
- Developing a communication policy that requires sending weekly announcements, recaps, or notices to parents via e-mail, e-newsletter, or web link allows for time to sit down, plan, develop, and send the communication.
- Campers and families love to see themselves in publications, and this creates buy-in and loyalty to the camp program, improving long-term sustainability among constituents.

Camp staff have many options for addressing a camper's homesickness. Effective methods will help the staff member build a relationship with the camper, demonstrating that camp can be a fun, safe, and caring place, even without the parents around.

If parents do not wish for the camp to call home in these instances, please inform a camp administrator and s/he will continue to work with the child throughout the camp experience. Additionally, parents of first-time campers suffering from separation anxiety should leave the child in our care rather than stick around to "phase out" the departure. This allows the staff to build a relationship with the child so the camper can see that camp is a fun, safe, and caring community, even when Mom and Dad aren't around.

If your child is ill on a scheduled day of camp, call the camp office to let staff know that he/she will not be attending. Children who become ill at camp will be sent home for the day.

Attire and Sunscreen

Camp is an active environment where children engage in sports and activities that may be dirty or messy. Please equip your child with appropriate attire that allows them to move safely, stay cool, and have fun. Proper footwear is essential to the safety and success of campers. Sneakers must be worn at all times. Open-toed shoes are allowed only in the pool area. Parents will be called and asked to bring appropriate footwear for their child in order for the camper to safely participate in the camp day.

Please make sure your child has sunscreen at all times, and pack extra if he/she needs an additional amount due to fair or sensitive skin. Please review with your child the dangers of sun exposure and let them know that if they need help applying sunscreen they should ask their counselors. Counselors will remind children to reapply sunscreen throughout the day.

Distribution of Medicine

The day camp staff cannot dispense over-the-counter medications to campers without consent from a parent. If your child would benefit from this type of medication, staff will call and discuss these options with you before dispensing any OTC meds to your child. Staff can dispense prescription medications provided the following conditions are met:

- A note from your child's doctor giving clear instructions for how the meds should be distributed.
- Informed consent from you allowing us to dispense the prescribed meds to your child.
- Medication is stored in the office, not your child's belongings.

- Medicine given to campers is documented by staff (see CD-ROM form 3.8: Medicine Log).

Children requiring accessibility to items such as inhalers and EpiPens will be allowed to have these items close at hand. These items must be given to the counselors, who carry a medical pack with the group at all times, for safe storage and distribution if and when required. Parents are encouraged to discuss these needs with their child's specific counselor, but parents should know that medical issues indicated on a camper's medical form are discussed with counselors prior to the camper's arrival in order for the counselor to prepare and plan for the accommodation of the needs of the individual with minimal impact on the larger group.

Conclusion

Developing camp polices is necessary for the successful implementation of any camp, new or old. Policies provide administrators, staff, campers, parents, and guardians with realistic expectations of what to expect from the camp beyond fun, safety, and child care. In addition, they offer protection to the camp when questions of behavior and judgment arise, provided the enforcement of the policy was consistent with legal statutes and incidents are documented. Policies must be updated annually to be successful year after year in a changing world. Additionally, policies must be clearly communicated to all those affected by policy enforcement. A good policy that is not shared is the same as having no policy at all.

Organizing the Camp Structure

Having surveyed the community, addressed safety issues, and established camp policies, you may believe you are ready to receive campers and begin your program. However, now is the time to organize your camp structure by planning and fine-tuning the registration process, reviewing and possibly changing your business plan, and revising the daily schedule based on changes that have occurred since you first developed it. Failing to organize the structure at this point can result in registration, financial, and scheduling problems that will ultimately affect the reputation of the program.

No matter what activities your camp program offers, you will need to revisit and revise your strategies along the way to achieve success.

Because of all the work you did at the beginning of the camp development process, you may believe that you have already addressed the issues discussed in this chapter. However, it is important to remember that some of those issues may have been drafted several months ago. As such, your initial projections and plans may no longer be relevant. Revisiting your work and addressing changes in camper numbers, group management (if camper numbers were lower or higher than projected), scheduling, facilities, resources, or personnel are essential to a successful first day of camp.

This chapter outlines suggestions for organizing registration, reviewing and changing the business plan according to the number of campers, if applicable, and organizing the daily program schedule based on changing camper numbers and group dynamics, or facility availability. These may seem like extra steps, but if you have developed plans for a new camp program based on a general idea, you would be wise to follow up now that you have more information. If you are working with an existing program, you may find that community interest in new activities may have increased or decreased. In either case, revisiting plans and making adjustments are essential to the success of your program.

Registration Process

Planning how to organize and manage the registration process is absolutely essential. Keep in mind that the registration process is patrons' first impression of the camp. Parents and guardians who feel good about the registration process will feel comfortable leaving their child in the care of camp staff. Registration should involve collecting all of the information necessary for providing fun and safe activities, including medical health forms and emergency contact information (see CD-ROM form 3.6: Health History). An easy, organized registration process will ease any anxiety parents and guardians may have about enrolling their children in the camp.

FORM 3.6

Health History

This form must be completed in full, including signatures of parent or legal guardian, and sent in by _____ to the camp office, located at _____. Campers will not be allowed to participate without the completed health and parental release forms.

Camp name _____

Date of camp _____

Camper's name _____ Gender _____

　　　　　　(Last)　　　　　　(First)

Age _____

Street address _____

City _____ State _____ Zip _____

Home phone (___) ___-_____ Height _____ Weight _____

Medical History (please check for "yes")

☐ German measles (Rubella)　☐ Scarlet fever　☐ Diabetes
☐ Measles　☐ Chicken pox　☐ Epilepsy
☐ Mumps　☐ Pneumonia　☐ Heart condition
☐ Other: _____　☐ Heat illness

Immunization History		Allergy History			Medication Allergies		
	Month/year		Yes	No		Yes	No
MMR	_____	Hay fever	☐	☐	Sulfa	☐	☐
Diphtheria	_____	Asthma	☐	☐	Penicillin	☐	☐
Tetanus	_____	Eczema	☐	☐	Antibiotic	☐	☐
Polio vaccine	_____	Insect stings	☐	☐	Other: _____		
Pertussis (whooping cough)	_____						

If your child will take medication during camp, indicate the name of the drug, the reason for taking it, the dosage, and the frequency:

_____

_____

From J. Moffitt, 2011, Day camp programming and administration: Core skills and practices (Champaign, IL: Human Kinetics). Adapted, by permission, from University of Vermont Campus Recreation.

Administrators often believe that a well-planned registration process will run itself with no hitches. Although this is true to some extent, it does not take much for even a well-planned registration process to break down. The following sections outline various registration processes, including advantages and disadvantages and tips for implementing them.

Online Registration

Online registration can be very convenient. Online tools range in price and capability, but most camps will be able to find a product that meets their needs and budget. Regardless of the product you select, the following suggestions will help you get the most out of it:

- Practice using the online tools that will be used for registration so that you can walk families through the registration process over the phone when questions arise.
- Save camp forms in a pdf format and e-mail them to families upon registration, or make them available for download online.
- Spend time with the online registration system. If you can't use it, don't expect families to be able to.
- Make sure you have a server that can handle the demand of the camp registration.
- Pay the extra money for a secure network.
- If possible, use a server, network, or process that is connected to the larger organization. If you must purchase online capability, make sure it will pay for itself through ongoing revenue generation.
- Check the system's financial reports regularly to make sure charges are going through and the camp is being charged the agreed amount to run credit cards.
- Have someone ready to speak to people who are struggling with registering online. Combining online convenience with a personal touch is the best way to provide online registration.
- Be patient with people who are hesitant to provide information online; encourage them to register online by talking about the secure features of the system, and offer to walk them through the process via telephone.
- Offer an alternative to online registration for those who are not computer savvy or do not have access to a computer.

Mail-In Registration

Despite the popularity and prevalence of computers and online shopping features, a few community members may still not be comfortable with purchasing camp sessions online. Providing a mail-in registration process in addition to an online one is one way to meet this need. If you cannot afford online registration, you may choose to use mail-in registration exclusively.

CAMP COUNSEL

Registration Host Sites

Following is a short list of host sites for camp registration. Typically, these sites help you set up the registration process. Families register for camp online and pay the host site directly, and the host site sends the camp a check for the amount earned online, minus the host site's fee. These sites are affordable alternatives to purchasing an online registration system, which can be too expensive for many new, small, or struggling camps.

- 123Signup: www.123signup.com (This site can also be used for event and membership management for the larger organization.)
- Active Network: www.campregister.com
- CampBrain: www.campbrain.com
- EZ-CAMP2: www.softerware.com/ezcamp2/
- Jackrabbit Camp: www.jackrabbitcamp.com

When using mail-in registration, consider the following:

- Make registration forms, medical forms, and photograph waivers clear, easy to read, and easy to understand (for examples, see CD-ROM form 3.1: Media and Photo Release for Minor Children, form 3.4: Kids Camp Registration, and form 3.6: Health History).
- Provide a telephone number on the materials for personal help.
- Make the camp address clear for mailing back payments.

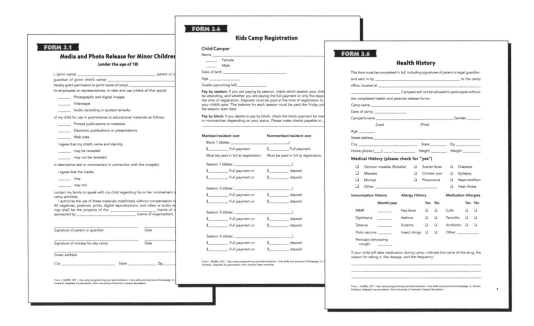

88

- On the form, provide a space for people to pay by credit card by filling in their information (camps requiring up-front payment or organizations not allowing the use of personal checks will need to do this).

- Follow up with patrons by letting them know you received the registration. This brings great peace of mind to patrons, and they are unlikely to forget your courtesy.

- Because mail-in processes are time-consuming, include an additional fee for processing mail-in registration forms (this encourages people to use the online tools and frees up your staff).

Walk-In Registration

Walk-in registration can supplement an online or mail-in registration process (or both) or serve as the only method of registration. This registration method has some advantages for camp administrators but may not be as user friendly as the other two methods. Walk-in registration requires the use of additional staff, who must be trained. Some larger organizations have customer service or information staff take care of walk-in camp registration. If you plan to do so, you should consider how that might affect the regular operations of the organization. Additionally, it is recommended to develop a checklist for these staff members to make sure that the full process of camp registration is being honored (for examples, see CD-ROM form 5.1: Walk-In Registration Checklist for Staff of a Larger Organization and form 5.2: Instructions for Helping Patrons Register Online). It is also a good idea to consider whether the advantages of walk-in registration outweigh the loss of convenience for patrons.

When using walk-in registration, consider the following:

- Having set hours for walk-in registration may be best for staff who are responsible for camp registration while maintaining other duties for the larger organization.

FORM 5.1

Walk-In Registration Checklist for Staff of a Larger Organization

When registering a patron for summer camp, be sure that the following forms are completed.

☐ Camp registration form
- All sections are complete.
- The total indicated on the form at the bottom matches the number of sessions registered.
- Lunch or snack options are complete and included in payment.
- Emergency contacts are listed.

☐ Health history form
- Immunization record is complete.
- Insurance information is complete.
- Allergies and special needs are indicated.
- Primary physician information is included.

Once you have reviewed the forms, follow these steps to complete the registration and payment process.

1. Write the camper's name in the group list that the patron registered for to secure the camper's place.
2. If the camper registered for lunch or snacks, include the camper's name in the lunch and snack section for each session registered.
3. Put the forms in the camp box.
4. After making sure the necessary requirements (below) are submitted by the patron to process payment, put cash, check, or credit card slip in the drawer and issue a receipt to the patron.

☐ Paid by check
- Driver's license number is on the check.
- Telephone number is on the check.
- Check is signed.

☐ Paid by cash

☐ Paid by credit card

From J. Moffit, 2011, *Day camp programming and administration: Core skills and practices* (Champaign, IL: Human Kinetics).

1

FORM 5.2

Instructions for Helping Patrons Register Online

When helping patrons register online, talk the patron through the following steps:

1. Have the patron go to the camp web site: _____

2. Tell the patron to click on the Register for Camp button located at: _____

3. Walk the patron through the sections of the online registration form, keeping in mind the following sections may require additional help:
- Lunch and Snack Options Reminders: _____
- Allergies and Special Needs Reminders: _____
- Selection of Camper Group Reminders: _____
- Be sure to inform the patron that requesting to be in the same group as another camper is allowed, although group requests cannot be guaranteed.
- Emergency Contact Reminders: _____
- Individuals Who CAN'T Pick Up the Camper Reminders: _____
- Other Camp Reminders: _____
_____
_____
_____
_____

4. Have the patron enter credit card information and click Submit. Registration is complete.

From J. Moffit, 2011, *Day camp programming and administration: Core skills and practices* (Champaign, IL: Human Kinetics).

2

- If walk-in registration is the only form of registration, consider identifying a date to open registration. Doing so allows you to make sure that you have enough staff and other resources to serve many patrons at once. A well-organized process and a limited registration period can make a great first impression on your camp constituency.

- The opportunity to meet a large number of campers and families should not be wasted. Walk-in registration offers the opportunity to develop strong relationships with members of the community.

- An additional fee for walk-in registration is recommended to encourage patrons to use the online tools and may be necessary because you must pay employees to process paperwork, which will increase staffing costs.

Transition Plan

A flexible registration policy that meets the needs of all patrons is recommended. However, in light of our society's growing commitment to going green, it is best to transition camper registrations, information, and other needs to secure online sites that are easy to navigate. Moving patrons from snail mail and walk-in registration to online registration will take time. Create a transition plan that gives patrons at least a year to migrate to online registration smoothly, and communicate it clearly to parents and guardians. One way to achieve this is to put notices on registration materials pointing patrons to the web site and giving an end date for when the camp will stop mail-in and walk-in registration and require patrons to register online. You could also send an e-mail to community members several months prior to registration, and again a couple of months after the camp season ends reminding patrons of your plan to transition from paper to online processes. For an example of a transition plan and sample content for notifications to patrons, see CD-ROM form 5.3: Transition Plan From Walk-In/Mail-In to Online Registration and form 5.4: Sample Content for Notifying Patrons of Transition Plan.

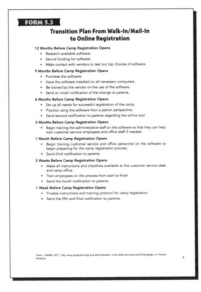

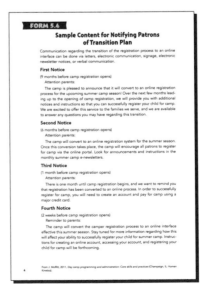

Business Plan

A business plan is a formal statement of the camp's goals, the reasons these goals are believed to be achievable, and the plan for reaching those goals. This section addresses the ingredients of the business plan necessary for reaching camp goals: fiscal responsibility and an effective organizational structure. A fictional financial blueprint example demonstrates how to turn a financial blueprint into a business plan that can be used for the duration of the summer camp. It begins with a cost analysis of expenses and line items that emerged during the development of the camp.

From Blueprint to Budget

In figure 5.1, the original costs (identified during the getting-started phase of camp development) are boldfaced, and the changed or added costs (costs that have changed for the camp since the getting-started phase) are italicized.

FINANCIAL BLUEPRINT

EXPENSES				INCOME		
	Projected	Realistic	Reason for change		Projected	Realistic
Wages	**$20,480.00**	*$21,120.00*	State minimum wage increased	**Week 1**	**$8,400.00**	*$9,600.00*
Wage fringe	**$1,638.40**	*$1,689.60*	Wages go up; fringe goes up	**Week 2**	**$8,400.00**	*$9,600.00*
Office supplies	**$300.00**	$300.00		**Week 3**	**$8,400.00**	*$9,600.00*
Equipment maintenance fees	**$300.00**	*$1,000.00*	Do not underestimate the wear and tear on equipment used by children.	**Week 4**	**$8,400.00**	*$9,600.00*
Miscellaneous expenses	**$500.00**	*$1,000.00*	Rapidly changing environment: double your original budget to be safe; you can always move unused money out.	**Week 5**	**$8,400.00**	*$9,600.00*

(continued)

Figure 5.1   The organization phase of administrative planning is the time to turn a blueprint financial plan into a working budget.

FINANCIAL BLUEPRINT *(continued)*

	EXPENSES				INCOME	
	Projected	**Realistic**	**Reason for change**		**Projected**	**Realistic**
Sports and games	**$1,000.00**	$1,000.00		**Week 6**	**$8,400.00**	*$9,600.00*
Swimming	**$200.00**	*$500.00*	Additional life vests needed	**Week 7**	**$8,400.00**	*$9,600.00*
Archery	**$1,500.00**	$1,500.00		**Week 8**	**$8,400.00**	*$9,600.00*
Adventure	**$2,000.00**	$2,000.00				
Field trips	**$6,480.00**	*$6,880.00*	Transportation costs raised by company; tied to gas prices	Miscellaneous income, late fees for payment plans, and retail sales should be included here if applicable; sales tax fees on all retail items may apply.		
Nature	**$500.00**	$500.00		**Total**	**$67,200.00**	*$76,800.00*
Environmental science	**$500.00**	$500.00				
Marketing	**$2,000.00**	*$4,000.00*	To make money, you have to spend money, so allow yourself to do that.			You can raise the price to cover the additional cost and still maintain the 80% profit per child, or you can decrease the profit margin.
Camp shirts	**$650.00**	**$650.00**				
Total	**$38,048.40**	*$42,639.60*				
		Income	**$67,200.00**	*$76,800.00*		
		Expenses	**$38,048.40**	*$42,639.60*		
		Profit	**$29,151.60**	*$34,160.40*		

Figure 5.1 *(continued)*

Because it is impossible to specify here the changes in funding and resources your particular camp might face, figure 5.1 looks at the most commonly changing and unplanned-for expenses. Typically, these include increased costs of wages, fringe benefits associated with wages, equipment, and field trips. Scrutinize every cost and make sure your plan is as realistic as possible so that you can manage your budget and achieve your targeted profit.

Once you have reviewed your initial financial blueprint and updated it where needed, you are ready to delegate the management of the financial plan to other members of the administrative staff, if applicable. Having one professional responsible for camp finances decreases confusion, miscommunication, and late payments and provides direct accountability. Although every member of the staff should be informed of the budget status periodically, the details should be the responsibility of one person who works with the programming administrator to meet the financial goals of the camp while providing high-quality programming.

To achieve success, you must spend money on camp needs long before registration begins and revenue is coming in. Facility-based camps that are intended to be self-sustaining or increase the profits of the larger organization may have difficulty obtaining start-up money. Existing programs that operate from a budget that rolls over from year to year, and that have access to monies from previous camp seasons, will have an easier time. In either case, monies are allocated and distributed in a variety of ways depending on the recreational sector to which the camp belongs.

Public sector camps may be funded from tax revenue of the town or city or may be eligible for state and federal grants. Private sector camps may receive funds from the larger organization. This investment acts like a start-up fund that the camp may or may not pay back based on its success. Nonprofit sector camps are often funded through fund-raising activities, donors, or federal and state grant monies, if eligible. Existing camp programs may decide to increase funds by raising camp costs or lowering camp expenses. Additionally, an existing program that decides to implement a new camp activity may be eligible for grant monies, sponsorships, or donor funds depending on the goals of the activity.

Camp Organization

The business plan should include the organizational structure of the camp. Much of what happens at camp, and who is responsible for it, can be easily communicated in a solid camp organizational chart coupled with job descriptions. Common duties for counselors, activity leaders, and the administrative staff (director and assistant director) appear next, and figure 5.2 shows a general organizational chart that can easily be modified for any camp. In the sample organizational chart, the counselor teams are divided up among the assistant directors as a way to manage and balance the workload of the assistants, as well as to give counselors a go-to administrator if they need anything. That is important for large camps, but small camps may not need that type of division. In that case, they would report to the assistant director of programs and facilities. These examples are not intended to be all-inclusive; rather, they provide a general starting place for structuring this part of your business plan. You will want to develop individual organizational charts and job descriptions for your own camp, because camps are unique. One size does not fit all.

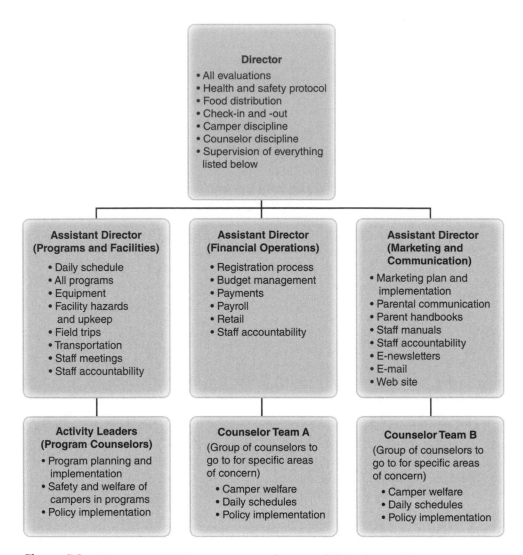

Figure 5.2 Camp organization structure and responsibilities by position.

General Camp Counselor

- **Job summary:** Directly supervise campers and assist in the instruction of activities. Youth day counselors are responsible for supervising and implementing preplanned activities on and off campus.

- **Job relationships:** Responsible to the administrative staff and for providing assistance to activity leaders during activity periods.

- **Job requirements:**
  - Strong interpersonal communication skills
  - Knowledge of the employee manual
  - Current certifications: CRP and first aid (all); professional lifeguard certification (aquatics only)

- o Ability to safely and efficiently work with all children from 6 to 13 years of age
- o Ability to be a role model for peers
- o Attendance of weekly staff meetings
- o Ability to take direction from activity leaders during program activities
- **Job responsibilities:**
  - o Ensure the safety and well-being of campers.
  - o Provide a nonthreatening atmosphere conducive to a positive social, creative, and athletic experience.
  - o Check group attendance and report tardy and absent children to the assistant director of programming.
  - o Closely supervise children in all group activities and while arriving and departing from all activities. Monitor locker rooms and supervise lunch hour and activity periods.
  - o Plan and prepare daily equipment needs.
  - o Assist activity leaders in setup, program delivery, and take-down of activities.
  - o Keep the equipment area, instructional facility, and fields clean and orderly.
  - o Turn in all paperwork on time and properly completed.
  - o Report problems, concerns, or suggestions to the assistant director immediately.
  - o Wrap up the day's activities with campers. Assist with parent pickup and make sure the group meeting area is clear of trash and lost articles of clothing before leaving.

Activity Leader

- **Job summary:** Directly organize, plan, and facilitate programming activities in the area assigned. This includes leading counselors and groups in planned activities.
- **Job relationships:** Responsible to the administrative staff member in charge of the specific program and required to organize and delegate roles to counselors assisting during activity periods.
- **Job requirements:**
  - o Strong interpersonal communication skills
  - o Knowledge of the employee manual
  - o Current certifications: CRP and first aid (all); professional lifeguard certification and WSI (aquatics only)
  - o Ability to safely and efficiently work with all children from 6 to 12 years of age
  - o Ability to delegate activity assignments to counselors
  - o Ability to be a role model for peers
  - o Attendance of weekly staff meetings

- **Job responsibilities:**
  - Ensure the safety and well-being of campers.
  - Provide all campers with a safe, enjoyable environment in which to learn and succeed.
  - Establish standards for campers, staff, and activities to provide for maximum safety, learning, and enjoyment.
  - Provide a nonthreatening atmosphere conducive to a positive social, creative, and athletic experience.
  - Plan activities to follow an established progression that will allow for the safest, most logical acquisition of skills.
  - Plan for and prepare daily equipment.
  - Create new and varied learning experiences, and document campers' success in those experiences so that parents and guardians can view their progress (aquatics).

The activity leader will plan activities that provide campers with a safe, enjoyable environment in which to learn and succeed.

- ○ Keep the equipment area, instructional facility, and fields clean and orderly.
- ○ Turn in all paperwork on time and properly completed.
- ○ Report problems, concerns, or suggestions to the assistant director of programming immediately.

Director

- **Job summary:** Responsible for all facets of the camp, including planning, policy development, staffing, staff training, program implementation, parental communication, fiscal accountability, and evaluation.
- **Job relationship:** Works for the larger organization and is held accountable for all facets of the camp program by the executive director (larger organizational leader) of the organization. Works collaboratively with other members of the larger organization to advance the mission and goals of the camp and the vision of the larger organization.
- **Job requirements:**
  - ○ CPR, first aid, and AED (automated external defibrillator) certification
  - ○ Excellent communication skills
  - ○ Demonstrated leadership abilities
  - ○ Effective strategic planning skills and the ability to plan, implement, and evaluate camp programs using appropriate and available tools
  - ○ Three or more years of experience in education or organized camping (combined experience preferred)
- **Job responsibilities:**
  - ○ Update and implement the emergency action plan, and train staff to implement the plan and act appropriately.
  - ○ Plan, organize, and facilitate counselor training.
  - ○ Provide ongoing counselor training and direction for staff.
  - ○ Assist in the administrative duties of check-in and checkout procedures.
  - ○ Draft disciplinary procedures and protocols.
  - ○ Train staff in, and implement, camper and staff disciplinary procedures.
  - ○ Prepare and lead weekly counselor meetings.
  - ○ Communicate regularly and accurately with administrative members regarding camp policies, campers, staff, programs, and other issues.
  - ○ Communicate effectively with staff, campers, and parents and guardians daily through the various communication tools available.
  - ○ Keep track of all purchases made during or leading up to camp (e.g., for programs, supplies, events, wages, reimbursements) to ensure an accurate and detailed financial picture.
  - ○ Operate the camp within the predetermined budget parameters.
  - ○ Communicate with parents and guardians on an ongoing basis via parent newsletter, registration process, and open house.

- Plan, organize, and implement the following programs on a daily basis:
  1. Field trips and special events for all groups
  2. All attendance sheets, daily reports, and incident reports
  3. Everything regarding the daily operations and business of the camp
- Assist and train administrative staff in all aspects of the programs they supervise.

Assistant Director (three positions)

- **Job summary:** Responsible for the programming, financial operations, and marketing and communication of the camp. Accountable to the director of the camp to serve as a resource and leader for one of three areas.
- **Job relationship:** Works on behalf of the camp organization to coordinate and implement programming activities and oversee financial considerations and marketing and communication strategies. Provides additional oversight and support for camp staff, serves as a liaison to families and campers on behalf of the director, and performs other duties as required.
- **Job requirements:**
  - Strong interpersonal communication skills
  - Knowledge of the employee manual
  - Current certifications: CRP and first aid (all)
  - Ability to safely and efficiently train and develop staff
  - Ability to delegate assignments to counselors
  - Exceptional work ethic
  - Strong leadership skills
  - Attendance of weekly staff meetings
- **Job responsibilities:**
  - Thoughtfully consider all programs, events, and activities, keeping safety as the number one priority.
  - Plan, organize, and facilitate counselor training.
  - Provide ongoing counselor training and direction for counselors and activity leaders.
  - Keep accurate records of participation numbers in all programs directly responsible for.
  - Assist in the administrative duties of check-in and checkout procedures.
  - Understand and responsibly implement camper and staff disciplinary procedures.
  - Prepare for and lead weekly counselor meetings.
  - Communicate regularly and accurately with administrative members regarding camp policies, campers, staff, programs, and other issues.
  - Assist in effectively communicating with parents, guardians, and counselors on a regular basis.
  - Assist in the programming, implementation, and coordination of other camps when required.

- Oversee the programming components of assigned programs.
- Plan, organize, and implement the following programs on a daily basis with other administrative staff members:
  1. Counselors-in-training
  2. Kids and fitness
  3. Team building
  4. Sports and games
  5. Pool programming
- Oversee all financial transactions related to the camp, including the following:
  1. Registration
  2. Program expenses
  3. Marketing and communication expenses
  4. Staff wages
  5. Contracted payments
  6. Miscellaneous expenses
  7. Refunds
  8. Projected profit
- Communicate with parents and guardians on behalf of the camp staff, the director, campers, and the larger organization when required.
- Oversee all marketing strategies employed across the community to brand the camp name and maximize participation.
  1. Web site
  2. Newsletters
  3. Advertisements (online, radio, and newspaper)
  4. E-mail communication
  5. Telephone communication
  6. Staff incentives and recognition

Staff Performance Standards

In addition to providing clear job descriptions that outline the roles of all camp staff, you need to identify and clearly communicate your expectations of the entire staff. Developing performance standards is essential in communicating the importance of staff members' roles in the camper experience. These standards also clarify for staff what is expected of them and what they will be evaluated on throughout the summer. Following is a short list of standards that may be applicable to any camp staff position:

- The major responsibility of camp staff is to ensure the safety and well-being of each camper. *No other duty should come in the way of following this prime directive.* Promptly enforce all rules and regulations, and stop all unsafe actions.
- Be aware and administer the engineering and work practice controls for the Blood-Borne Pathogens Occupational Exposure Plan.

CAMP COUNSEL ▬▬▬▬▬▬▬▬

Specialty Jobs in Facility-Based Camps

Other jobs that are common in camps are lifeguards and counselors-in-training. Lifeguards and aquatic, or waterfront, directors need well-defined job descriptions that list the duties of the position and the associated responsibilities for providing safe water activities. Following are general items to consider in a lifeguard or aquatic job description:

- List the minimal certifications and experience required for lifeguards or aquatic directors.
- List preferred certifications and qualifications, if applicable.
- List the ages of the campers the person will supervise and create programs for.
- List the number of groups the person will be responsible for supervising and programming for throughout the day.
- Indicate whether the person in this position will have responsibilities at camp when no aquatic activity is taking place (e.g., will he or she be required to be an additional counselor in a group).
- Indicate whether weekly lesson plans are required and how much time the person will have to create those plans.
- Indicate the requirement for camper swim tests and the person's responsibility to manage poor swimmers and keep them safe in the water.
- Include the duties associated with swim lessons that are part of the daily schedule and the level of organization, testing, and skill development that is expected in teaching children to swim while at camp.

Counselors-in-training (CITs) are underage teens who come to camp to learn what it takes to work with children. The advantage for the CIT is a hands-on experience in a camp setting that keeps them busy over the summer months and helps position them for a job when they become old enough to work at camp. The advantage for the camp is extra eyes and hands to help supervise and set up during camp programming. CIT job descriptions require clear boundaries because these young people are also considered a vulnerable population that the camp is required to protect. This charge requires specific rules for what CITs can and cannot do when providing additional help and supervision to younger campers. Research state laws and legislation regarding the requirements for serving vulnerable populations before outlining a job description for CITs in your program.

- *Know where your group members are.* Closely supervise children during all activities including lunch, field trips, and walking to and from events. Understand the value of head counts, and practice them often.
- Meet and communicate with parents and guardians. Inform them about what took place during the day and how their children performed.

Staff performance standards clarify for staff what is expected of them.

- Ensure the safety of the facility and equipment during your preparation for all activities.
- Ensure that the group meeting area is clean and free of trash before leaving for the day.
- Help with camper drop-off before camp and camper pickup after camp. Ensure that every child leaves with an authorized person(s) as indicated by the parents or guardians on the camper check-in and checkout forms provided. (See CD-ROM form 4.5: Camper Check-In and Checkout.)
- Report and document all emergency or injury situations to the administrative staff and on an incident or accident report. (See CD-ROM form 4.11: Camper Incident Report.)
- *Under no circumstances* is a child or group to be left unattended (if you are outside and a child needs to use the restroom, escort him or her to and from the restroom).
- Be willing and ready to help out any member of the camp when required.

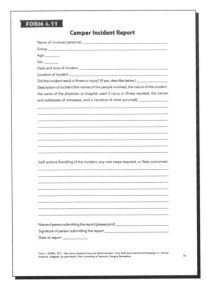

Daily Program Schedule

Changes that occurred during the registration process, and financial changes that affect the availability of facilities and equipment, will require that you revisit the daily program schedule, as well as your inventory of equipment and materials. Your best plan is to engage in this process during group formation.

Although finances and equipment are important factors in planning camp offerings and designing daily schedules, the largest dictator of daily schedules is the number of campers that register. This number affects the way groups are formed, the number of groups, the demographics of the groups, and the size of the groups, all of which play important roles in the successful implementation of a daily schedule.

Anticipating changes in facilities, financial resources, registration processes, and equipment needs may be easy as plans for the upcoming summer season progress. This is generally true for both new camps and existing camps. More difficult to anticipate, particularly for new programs, is the number of campers that will actually register for the camp, week to week. Even more difficult for new programs is trying to plan for the wide range of ages that register, which affects staffing needs and training, group management, and ultimately the daily schedule. Existing programs can often anticipate the number of campers based on past camp seasons. Younger programs that are still building the camp may find similar challenges as new camp programs in dealing with unanticipated camper numbers.

Camper-Number Outcomes

If your camp is new or young, a few strategies will help you be as prepared as possible. Generally speaking, camper numbers have three potential outcomes for driving the implementation of the camp—worst case, best case, and in-between case.

First, consider the possibility that you do not reach your camper target number, and develop a plan for the minimal number of campers. Ask yourself how many campers you will need per group, how many staffing changes you will have to make to adhere to that number, and what minimal changes to the schedule will be required to make the best use of your resources without devaluing the camp experience. This is a worst-case adjustment plan.

Likewise, you should develop a plan for achieving a maximum number of participants, or a best-case adjustment plan. This plan considers staffing needs, program equipment and materials, and adjustments to the daily schedule. If your camp fills up and campers are on a wait list, you might be tempted to allow additional campers in to increase profits. However, if the camp is not prepared for more campers and the potential issues they invite, opt for maintaining your reputation and deny access. Having a highly valued camp is the goal, and putting profits over long-term sustainability and safety can ruin a camp in one summer. An existing program that makes such a mistake can rely on its forged relationships to mitigate the problem. A problem such as this in a camp's first season, however, creates a first impression that may be impossible to overcome.

The final potential outcome of camper numbers is the in-between case, in which the number of registered campers is close to the number of anticipated campers on which the plans were constructed. This situation may require adjustments to schedules if resources, equipment, or staffing issues have emerged in the interim. Often, new camp programs make the mistake of assuming that because reality matched their plan, they are in good shape. As a result, they may fail to make the adjustments required to correctly group campers, change schedules, train staff, or modify staff numbers based on the numbers of campers who registered and the final camper demographic. The in-between plan might be the best scenario you can hope for, but attention to organizing camp needs based on changing resources is still required.

Grouping Strategies

When the campers who enroll represent a wide age range, mistakes in grouping can occur. Luckily, these are easily corrected as long as you adhere to the recommended camper-to-counselor ratio. Existing programs may face this challenge, but once again, they have the advantage of community relationships and camp history to help them negotiate these waters. Furthermore, most long-established camp programs have already worked out a system for age-appropriate grouping over time and from experience. This section provides solutions for new programs that end up with age ranges that are either highly varied or not varied enough.

Grouping by School Grades

Grouping children together who are within one grade of each other, and giving groups names associated with these grades, is ideal, if possible. The names are important in how the group will be known at camp and allows campers to invest in their shared group experience in a more meaningful way. Here is an example of three groups:

- Rattlers: Rising first- and second-graders
- Cardinals: Rising third- and fourth-graders
- Royals: Rising fifth- and sixth-graders

Because camp happens in the summer, you will need to determine whether to base groups on the grades campers just completed, their birth dates, or the grades they are moving (rising up) to. Using rising grades highlights the development of individual children rather than their actual ages. The assumption is that educators who work with children regularly throughout the year are more qualified than camp administrators to determine their developmental levels. Although this rule cannot be used every time for every child, it is a good starting place. In some cases, the biological age and physical development may be more appropriate for grouping children at camp than their cognitive developmental age as determined by the school. In these cases, you may want to determine the best location for campers on an individual basis and with input from the campers and their families.

Multiple Same-Age Groups

If you have an overabundance of campers of a certain age or level, you may need to create two or three groups for them. Let's say, for example, that you plan to have one group of campers in the rising second-grade group. However, the number of second-graders who register is double what you expected. As a result, you form

Grouping children by school grade is a good idea, but you also need to keep in mind their individual developmental levels.

two groups of second-graders. This may require that you reorganize some portions of the daily schedule to serve two groups of children in this grade.

Be advised that parents, guardians, and campers will request group placements. Friends will want to be with friends, siblings with siblings, neighbors with neighbors, and so on. These requests should be accommodated, if reasonable, meaning that they are in line with age-appropriate or developmentally appropriate guidelines and do not affect the larger group. These requests should not be guaranteed. You may find that a trial basis for the most overzealous camper family is the best short-term solution that can lead to a long-term placement depending on the success of the trial.

"Tweener" Groups

You may find yourself with a number of campers in a "tweener" stage, meaning that they are physically too old, but cognitively too young, for their rising grades, or vice versa. Creating a group for these campers on the cusp of developmental levels requires constant communication with staff and parents and guardians.

You may identify potential tweeners when reviewing the medical release forms and parents' and guardians' comments. If a registration form lacks the information you need to place a child, you might ask parents or guardians for more information, explaining that you need it to place the child appropriately. Let them know that campers may not be placed in permanent groups until the second day of camp because adjustments to groups are common. You should also identify potential tweeners to camp staff and ask them to observe these children during the first day of camp to help determine whether they would appropriately be grouped in a tweener group. It is possible that a tweener group could replace a group from your initial plan, but tweener groups are more commonly added to the groups and will need to be accommodated.

Luckily, tweeners are successful at camp when they share schedules or activity times with other groups. For example, a tweener group consisting of campers who are physically too old for their rising grade would do quite well participating in a sport or game with the age group directly ahead of them. Likewise, they would be successful participating in environmental science education activities with a group directly behind them. This minimizes changes to the daily schedule (staff should plan for the group on the schedule that is not a tweener group). In fact, you may be able to develop a schedule for a tweener group without having to make any adjustments to facility schedules or pool times. This solution is best used with biologically older camper groups. Be sure to choose a name for this group that is more appropriate than "tweener," which some may find derogatory.

Triple-Age Groups

You may decide to group very large, but controllable, age ranges in threes, such as rising first-graders to rising third-graders. This is the concept behind traditional middle schools, so it might work well for very small camps or new camps depending on the closeness and size of the community. Triple-age groups are not ideal because children's developmental levels vary a great deal within three years in all four learning domains (cognitive, physical, affective, and social). However, if cancelling the camp is counterproductive to building a program that serves the community and the organization, then grouping campers in this way may be your

Tweener Power

While working at a camp in the Southwest in 2000, I was faced for the first time with the prospect of developing an entire camper group made of tweeners. I was unsure of how to work out the schedule and how to train staff to handle a larger range of ages, and I was nervous about having conversations with parents about why their children would be placed in an intellectually and socially slower group when they could physically achieve locomotive skills at a level reserved for groups two grades higher than them. Perhaps my anxiety about the parental conversations got the better of me at that point in my career, but I decided to avoid that scenario altogether. I decided four things: 1) I would not tell anyone that it was a tweener group and avoid the parental conversations; 2) I would staff the group with individuals who had experience working with that age range—like lifeguards, swim instructors, and day care providers—so as to be able to get away with less staff training (remember this was my first time); 3) I would provide training on all of the stages of child development in the social, cognitive, physical, and affective domains of behavior and learning; and 4) I would include the tweener group with other groups to avoid scheduling issues by following the simple rule that tweeners would participate with a grade below in intellectually and affectively challenging activities and participate with a grade above in socially and physically challenging activities. I had no idea if these were the right decisions, so I agreed to be flexible and to solicit feedback from counselors and other staff as the summer started in order to make adjustments. To my amazement, my plan worked on all levels for a majority of the tweener campers. However, because I remained flexible and was open to feedback, I was able to satisfy the needs of those tweener campers for whom this set up did not work by allowing them to choose which group (one below or one above) they wanted to permanently join. My one big, although not fatal, mistake was not being as open with parents about the goals of the tweener group. Had I implemented a communication policy like the one I employ now, I would have been able to establish good relationships with those families and be honest about why I thought their children belonged in the tweener group (which by the way, was called the Bullfrogs, by their own choosing). That summer I had one conversation with a parent who indicated that all parents really want to know is why their kids are placed in a certain group and that most parents, if told why in an honest and sincere way, would trust the camp professionals' judgment. For me, it was a great lesson in community responsibility and the rights of the parents and the campers. The following summer, I disclosed the idea behind the tweener group and actually had parents request it for their child, which was very helpful and resulted in a successful tweener group for all campers enrolled. It was also much easier to group these kids and have honest conversations with parents who also just wanted the best for their children—at whatever level their children may have been.

only option. This solution should be implemented only as a last resort and when marketing initiatives and resources have been exhausted.

Program Cancellations

A final consideration for administrators is cancelling the camp program when the numbers or age levels do not make the camp viable or practical for the community. Cancelling the camp is recommended if holding it is not likely to produce a meaningful benefit to the camp, the campers, and the organization. If the major goal of the camp is to generate revenue, and a cost-benefit analysis indicates a staggering loss of the initial funding, then the camp should be cancelled. If, on the other hand, an analysis indicates a minimal financial loss, and the camp is supported by the larger organization or community, then, if possible, run the camp to get it started and begin building its reputation.

When faced with this decision, you must be comfortable with a reasonable amount of financial loss for at least three years before the camp begins to sustain itself and ultimately return a profit. The quickest way to kill a camp program is to terminate it prematurely. If you decide to hold the camp despite low numbers and a minimal financial loss, commit to a three- to five-year investment (or loss). Should the camp operate responsibly and innovatively, and change with the needs of the community, for more than 10 years, the camp, the organization, and the community will not be displeased with the return on that initial investment.

Conclusion

Changing needs, demographics, and resources are common threads in the camp development process. Through a well-planned and -organized registration process and a solid business plan that includes fiscal accountability and a well-thought-out camp organizational structure, you will be well positioned to accept campers and meet families on the first day of camp. This is especially true when your camp policies (see chapter 4) are coupled with the camp structure.

Preparing for opening day requires that you review and fine-tune your registration process, choosing a system that best meets the needs of your patrons, while ultimately moving them toward an online system. You will also need to review the costs of your programs and activities and identify how you will fund them. Finally, you may need to seek solutions to camper number and group formation issues.

Preparing for a number of grouping scenarios when planning a new camp or camp activities positions you well to handle the needs of the community once registration is complete. As noted in previous chapters, serving the community's needs is the fastest and most effective way to build a strong camp for years to come. Additionally, understanding the camp structure will help you train your staff. Staffing issues related to facility-based day camps are discussed in the next chapter.

Staffing the Camp

Staffing is the most important consideration for any facility-based day camp. Camp leaders are completely dependent on staff to ensure that all policies, programs, and risk management strategies are followed to provide high-quality programming while keeping campers safe. For this reason, you need to hire, train, and develop a qualified staff that advances the goals and mission of the camp. This chapter addresses staff qualifications, hiring procedures, training, ongoing development, performance evaluations, and counselor-in-training programs.

Qualifications

Developing a qualified staff begins with identifying the minimal qualifications to be considered for employment. The basic qualifications of a good camp employee should include a desire to work with children, experience working with children, and minimal certifications to meet the safety standards of federal and state laws and the larger organization.

Desire to Work With Children

People wishing to apply for a camp position may believe they need experience working with children to be considered. Although such experience may be preferred, it doesn't need to be a requirement. Those entering the camping world for the first time may not have worked with children. This is particularly true of high school students and first-year college students looking to gain experience with children for a variety of reasons including fun, future career plans, or just a general appreciation of children. What is most important for first-time counselors and camp staff is a genuine desire to work with children and develop relationships with them. This desire, rather than experience, should be a primary qualification for potential camp staff.

A desire to work with children is, of course, a subjective qualification and therefore difficult to evaluate. What you can glean about candidates from their applications and from phone or in-person conversations can help you determine whether they have this desire. Instinctive, or gut, feelings you may have from written or verbal communications are legitimate qualitative tools for evaluating potential hires in this regard.

Experience Working With Children

Your next decision about staff qualifications is how much experience working with children you want job candidates to have. The preceding section suggested that people with no experience working with children can be considered for staff positions as long as they demonstrate a genuine interest. This may not be enough for some camps depending on the laws that govern their location or the expectations of the larger organization.

Experience working with children can include babysitting jobs, student teaching experience, working in day care and after-school programs, taking care of younger siblings or relatives, working at amusement parks where contact with children is an everyday occurrence, working at establishments where children's parties are a staple (e.g., Chuck E. Cheese's, Celebration Station, Putt-Putt Golf), or simply planning programs that are relevant to children such as birthday parties. You may decide that one or two babysitting jobs provide adequate experience with children or require that candidates have a year of experience working in an organization that provides programs for children. You could also accept any combination of experience.

The larger organization may dictate what qualifies as experience working with children. If it is determined that at least one summer of experience working with children is required to be considered for a camp position, you can expect the candidate pool to be good, but small, because this requirement will limit the number of applications you receive.

Minimal Certifications

Determining what certifications counselors, activity and specialty leaders, administrative staff, aquatic staff, and health or infirmary staff must have to work at your camp will be dictated by the needs of the your clientele, federal and state laws governing the camp, the larger organization's requirements, field and best practice standards, and the programming needs of the camp. Additionally, you will need to determine whether to require that staff have these certifications prior to being hired, or whether they can obtain them after they are hired and before camp starts. In the latter case, you must decide who will pay for certifications, the employees themselves or the camp.

New programs should require that all counselors be certified in CPR, first aid, and AED (automated external defibrillator) by the time camp starts. Because some applicants will have these certifications and some will not, it is reasonable to prefer those who already have these certifications but be willing to pay for those who do not. This decision is affected by the budget, but generally it is a minimal cost and a worthwhile investment in camper safety. It is further recommended that these be the only certifications the camp pays for. More skill-based certifications necessary for waterfront activities, pools, behavior intervention, health care provision, and other specialty programs should be required of staff prior to hiring. These certifications are typically more expensive, and paying for them can become very costly.

Hiring Procedures

Creating hiring procedures is an important part of the camp development process. By considering your programming initiatives, risk management strategies, and camp policies, you can develop a hiring procedure that attracts strong applicants with diverse perspectives, experiences, and contributions. Hiring procedures address recruitment, the application process, the interview process, and the necessary paperwork including background checks.

Recruitment

Recruiting high-quality candidates is an important step toward ensuring that the camp program operates safely. Despite the temptation to post jobs and wait for candidates to apply, you would be well served to actively recruit the type of candidates you want.

Actively recruiting candidates who can develop good relationships with campers can help you to find the best person for the job.

Organizations and resources in your community may be good places to recruit staff. On college campuses, doing presentations in education classes, physical education classes, student minority clubs, and student organizations is an ideal way to spread the message about your camp program. Many students have an array of experiences working with children and can help the camp reach its goals. Education majors, social work majors, psychology majors, political science majors, business majors, and family and consumer science majors are great populations to recruit. To reach a larger, more diverse student population, you can use presentations, flyers, and other marketing strategies to target minority groups or special interest organizations in the community (Cronin, 2009). A phone call to the leader of any one of these groups can get the camp on a meeting agenda for 5 to 10 minutes to talk about the program, its impact on community youth, employees' influence in making a difference in campers' lives, and the ways it can benefit people on various career paths.

If you work in a private organization or municipality, you have similar resources available in the larger community, such as high schools. Today's high schools have many of the same types of organizations as colleges. Future educators, sociology, psychology, sport, minority group, and career-specific clubs, as well as the gay/straight alliance, are just some of the places you can recruit camp staff. In addition to high schools, businesses that sponsor the camp can be powerful allies in the hunt for a summer staff. A personal reference from a local business that you have a relationship with can make you feel comfortable offering the person an interview. Furthermore, local business partners can play a role in marketing summer staff positions and the camp program to the larger community.

Community organizations and local businesses can give you a better understanding of what the community workforce has to offer and how you can best put that force to use. Evaluating the skills of this workforce requires a strong application process that is functional but not rigid.

Applications

The employment application form should include the basic items needed by the organization, such as contact information, past experience, education, and references. However, a camp application must go beyond basic information gathering. It should include specific questions about work with children; skills; their philosophies about camp, education, and discipline; and how they would respond to certain scenarios. Answers to these types of questions offer insight as to whether the applicant has the minimal skills required to work at camp (see CD-ROM form 6.1: Employment Application).

Applicants should include a resume and cover letter with their applications, because these reveal applicable or transferrable skills that may be important additions to the camp program. The attention an applicant gives to the look and language of the entire application will give you a good sense of whether the person pays attention to details, follows instructions, and considers the job a serious employment opportunity. People who forget to include portions of the application, do not proofread, make many errors, or generally rush through the process indicate that the quality of their work may not meet your expectations. A well-thought-out application process is likely to attract qualified people who are serious about the job.

FORM 6.1

Employment Application

Full name _____ Date _____

    (Last)   *(First)*   *(M.I.)*

Street address _____

City _____ State _____ Zip _____

Phone (___) ___-_____ Summer e-mail _____

Date available _____ Social security no. _____ Desired salary _____

Position applying for _____ (counselor, activity leader,

lifeguard, assistant director)

                                   Yes   No

❑   Are you a citizen of the United States?   ❑   ❑

❑   If no, are you authorized to work in the United States? ❑   ❑

❑   Have you ever worked for this company?   ❑   ❑

❑   If yes, when? _____

❑   Have you ever been convicted of a felony?   ❑   ❑

❑   If yes, explain: _____

Education

High school _____

Address _____

From _____ to _____ Did you graduate? ❑ Yes ❑ No

College _____

Address _____

From _____ to _____ Did you graduate? ❑ Yes ❑ No

Degree _____

Other educational institution _____

Address _____

From _____ to _____ Did you graduate? ❑ Yes ❑ No

Degree _____

From J. Moffitt, 2011, Day camp programming and administration: Core skills and practices (Champaign, IL: Human Kinetics). Adapted, by permission, from University of Vermont Campus Recreation.

Interviews

Interviews give you a chance to meet and greet candidates. Because just about anything can happen at camp, you want the best possible picture of the kind of employee the person will be. Interview questions should include scenario questions to ascertain how candidates would handle themselves and the group in various situations (see CD-ROM form 6.2: Interview Tips and Sample Questions). You should also ask about the person's experience, references, strengths and weaknesses, and ability to work with others.

Interviews with potential staff should include several members of the administrative staff to provide a balanced perspective. Give each interviewer an interview screening form (see CD-ROM form 6.3: Interview Screening) to complete and submit to the director after each interview. The written thoughts of everyone on

FORM 6.2

Interview Tips and Sample Questions

1. The ability to put the needs of others ahead of your own. Good camp counselors are constantly caring for the youth in their charge. This means identifying the needs of others and attending to them without being distracted by one's own needs.

2. The ability to do the right thing and take a stand for what is true. Working with children is a privilege, and camp is a special place where campers get to play and grow in exceptional ways. Protecting camp by maintaining certain important rules requires a sense of leadership, and one element of leadership is taking a stand for what you believe, even if it is unpopular with your peers.

3. Another crucial ability for counselors is conflict resolution. Whether with campers or co-counselors, knowing how to resolve the many inevitable conflicts that arise on a daily basis at camp is crucial to strong performance.

4. And the last but certainly not the least important ability, or competence, is the capacity to work hard for long periods. Most camp counselors new to the position don't realize how taxing the work is until they go through a summer season!

Ditter, B. (2001). A key set of skills for counselors: In the trenches. Camping Magazine 74 (3), 12-14 (ERIC Document Reproduction Service No. EJ 627027).

1. Tell me about a time when you put the needs of another or others ahead of your own. Probing questions: What was the situation? What was the relationship between you and the person/people? How did you handle the situation? What did you learn? How did it go?

2. Tell me about a time when you took a stand for (or stood up for) something you believed in, even though it was an unpopular position. Probing questions: What was the stand you took? What was the principle or who was the person you stood up for? What did you do and say? What resistance or negative feedback did you encounter, and how did you handle it? What was the outcome? Looking back on it, what do you think about what you did or didn't do?

3. Tell me about a time when you had a conflict with a friend, employer, or authority of some kind (teacher, parent, coach). Probing questions: What was the conflict? Who was involved? What did you do? What was the outcome? What did you learn from the situation?

4. Tell me about a project in school, something you've had to do around the house, or some job you've had or volunteered for that took much more effort than you originally thought it would. Probing questions: What was the situation? How did you deal with it? What things did you actually do or say that helped you through it? What was the outcome?

5. Include three competency-based questions that are based on the essential competencies the camp leaders believe are necessary for success at camp.

Ditter, B. (1995). New directions in staff training and development. Camping Magazine, 67 (3), 38-42 (ERIC Document Reproduction Service No. EJ 505585).

From J. Moffitt, 2011, Day camp programming and administration: Core skills and practices (Champaign, IL: Human Kinetics).

FORM 6.3

Interview Screening

Name _____

Position _____

Camp _____

Relevant education _____

Relevant experience _____

_____

_____

❑   On time for interview

❑   Easy to talk to

❑   Good eye contact

❑   Asked pertinent questions

Comments: _____

_____

_____

_____

_____

Overall interview impression: _____

_____

_____

_____

_____

_____

Recommendation

❑   Hire without hesitation ❑   Hire with caution ❑   Do not hire

Interviewer (administrative staff member) signature _____

Camp director _____

Date _____

From J. Moffitt, 2011, Day camp programming and administration: Core skills and practices (Champaign, IL: Human Kinetics). Adapted, by permission, from University of North Carolina, Asheville Campus Recreation.

the interview team help the administrative staff decide which candidates to hire and also provide a variety of perspectives on skill sets that may or may not be appropriate for the camp.

Background Checks and Other Paperwork

Because of the vulnerability of the camp population, the final step of the hiring process is to complete background checks and other necessary paperwork. Some camps run background checks on all applicants, which can be expensive depending on the number of applicants. A better solution may be to run background checks on only the people the camp wishes to hire, with a caveat that employment is based on passing the check when the job is offered.

Another solution is to require that applicants pay for their own background checks when they apply for the job. This relieves the camp of any expense associated with checks. This solution may turn off applicants who cannot or do not want to pay for a background check.

Other paperwork required to work at camp will be determined by the laws, rules, and regulations that govern the camp at the state and organizational levels. Staff should complete the required paperwork prior to the start of training so that they are positioned to be compensated for their work without delay.

<u>Training</u>

Once the staff roster has been filled, training the staff is the next step. A one-week training period should adequately prepare your staff for the work ahead (see CD-ROM form 6.4: Counselor Training Outline). Staff training week is the most important tool for securing campers' safety, providing the staff with the skills, resources, and confidence required to work effectively (Ball & Ball, 1995; Ditter, 1995). Despite all your work planning for emergencies, developing waiv-

FORM 6.4

Counselor Training Outline

Time	Activity
9:00 a.m.	Meet
	Introductions
9:30 a.m.	Ice breakers
10:00 a.m.	Expectations, goals, manual
11:00 a.m.	Break
11:15 a.m.	Blood-borne pathogens
11:45 a.m.	Ice breaker
12:00 p.m.	Lunch
1:00 p.m.	Breakout sessions:
1:00-1:30 p.m.	Counselors assigned to individual age groups meet to discuss daily schedules and begin the co-counselor relationship.
1:30-2:00 p.m.	Counselors begin program brainstorming specific to team building and New Games activities.
2:00 p.m.	Break
2:15 p.m.	Sexual harassment training
2:45 p.m.	All-camp program on tennis courts
3:15 p.m.	Review tomorrow's agenda and Q&A
3:30 p.m.	Dismissed

Time	Activity
9:00 a.m.	Dance studio
9:30 a.m.	Designing innovative games (practical applications)
10:00 a.m.	Transition times
10:30 a.m.	Break
10:45 a.m.	Team-building activity
11:00 a.m.	Developing positive group dynamics
11:30 a.m.	Discipline procedures
12:00 p.m.	Modifying behaviors (practical applications)
12:45 p.m.	Ice breaker
1:00 p.m.	Lunch
2:00 p.m.	Diversity
3:00 p.m.	Emergency procedures, first aid kits, radio codes
3:30 p.m.	Administrative paperwork
3:45 p.m.	Team-building activity
4:00 p.m.	Field trips and special events and resources
4:15 p.m.	Quick overview of the daily schedule as a lead-in for tomorrow
4:30 p.m.	Counselors dismissed; activity leader breakout sessions
5:30 p.m.	Activity leaders dismissed

This is a program training day; all areas will be led by the activity leader and an administrative supervisor.

From J. Moffitt, 2011, *Day camp programming and administration: Core skills and practices* (Champaign, IL: Human Kinetics). Adapted, by permission, from University of Vermont Campus Recreation.

ers, creating health plans, and hiring the staff, the true success of your camp lies entirely in the hands of the frontline workers—your counselors.

CAMP COUNSEL ▮▮▮▮▮▮▮▮▮▮▮▮▮▮▮▮▮▮▮▮▮▮▮▮▮▮

Stages of Group Development

Developing positive group dynamics in camper groups is an important part of the role of camp staff. Small group development occurs in five stages, according to Tuckman and Jensen (1977): forming, norming, storming, performing, and adjourning. The stages described next apply Tuckman's expertise to camp staff.

Stage 1: Saying Hello
- Campers may be feeling insecure and unsure of themselves.
- Counselor's role: Clarify expectations, comfort them by talking about the camp and what there is to look forward to throughout the week, avoid personal feelings or close physical contact, and use name games and ice breakers to keep the group active.

Stage 2: Saying Who
- Campers will be sorting it all out, picking friends, developing roles in the group, and getting to know how the counselor works (what they can get away with!).
- Counselor's role: Watch for power struggles and cliques, encourage openness and sharing, help with conflict resolution, mix up the groups to separate certain campers, and use cooperative games.

Stage 3: Saying Why
- Campers understand their roles, are building a team, start to depend on each other, begin to work and share space together, and challenge leadership.
- Counselor's role: Help campers assume responsibility for their actions and decisions, help them solve problems and work out group decisions, and use team-building games and group activities.

Stage 4: Saying We
- Campers start to acknowledge each other's individual strengths, develop respect for each other, become interdependent, find success in their contribution to the group, and start sharing feelings with the group.
- Counselor's role: Allow time for creativity and discussion, provide group challenges and adventures, watch for exhaustion, and acknowledge individual and group accomplishments.

Stage 5: Saying Good-Bye
- Campers have mixed feelings about leaving camp, recognize the growth and change in themselves, and want to maintain ties with the camp and others in the group.
- Counselor's role: Encourage reflection, reward accomplishments, and help campers transfer what they learned to home and school after camp is complete.

Staff training sessions also give staff members the chance to develop relationships and positive group dynamics prior to the arrival of the campers. A community of caring can be created through well-structured team-building activities and initiatives during training week. This is important because positive group dynamics and supportive relationships with coworkers and supervisors can motivate staff throughout the summer months. Supported and happy staff members perform better and are more likely to meet the goals of the camp (Walton, 2001). During staff training, staff members also learn daily procedures, such as time sheet completion (see CD-ROM form 6.5: Time Sheet) and requests for time off (see CD-ROM form 6.6: Request for Time Off), among others.

Preparation for staff training week should take place in the initial stages of camp planning. The needs assessment and resource identification that happened at the beginning of this process will inform decisions about training, developing, and retaining the staff. Determining exactly what to cover and how to schedule training can be challenging and ultimately depends on the camp's goals, resources, and requirements. Generally, staff training should address discipline, camp protocols, safety, child development, and parental communication.

You should be very intentional about the plans for the first day of training. This day is crucial for selling the program, making staff members comfortable, and highlighting the ways working at the camp will help develop them as whole people. By the end of the first day, staff members should feel good about their work at the camp, their team, and the camp.

Standard Training Topics

Consider the camp's goals, resources, mission, and programming components, as well as community feedback, when determining the topics to cover during staff training. Although camps have unique requirements for training their staff,

Staff training is important for providing the staff with the skills, resources, and confidence required to work effectively.

there are many staple topics that every camp should consider, such as the camp mission, vision, values, goals, and expectations, and discipline procedures for staff infractions.

Begin staff training week by reviewing the camp mission, vision, values, and goals to set the stage for presenting the purpose of the camp and the difference the staff can make in the lives of community youth. A fundamental understanding of, and agreement with, the overall purpose of the camp will help the staff enforce policies, run programs, and follow safety protocols.

The next task of staff trainers is to describe the positions at the camp and how they advance the mission and goals. This is only a quick review because the staff should already be familiar with the job descriptions from the application and hiring processes. Spend time describing the work expectations of the staff (refer to chapter 5 for more details) to clearly communicate performance standards. Follow this with a review of the counselor discipline protocol. This protocol is usually dictated by the larger organization of a facility-based camp and as such will vary from camp to camp.

Additional Training Topics

Additional staff training topics include bullying, tips for becoming a successful counselor, leadership in the 21st century, learning styles, transitional times, innovative games, and conflict resolution. The first four topics are addressed in

CD-ROM form 6.7: Bullying Scenarios, form 6.8: Becoming a Successful Counselor, form 6.9: Leadership, and form 6.10: Learning Styles. The latter three are outlined briefly next.

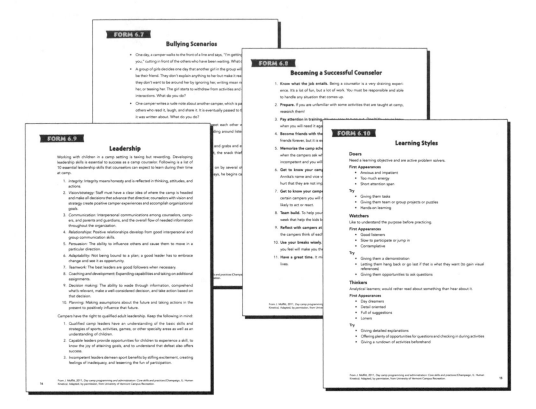

Transitional Times

Several transitional times naturally occur in camp daily schedules. These times are especially important for camp counselors to manage because they invite campers to make poor behavior choices out of inactivity and boredom. For example, lining up to move from one activity to another can be very difficult for young children (ages five to seven) if it takes too long. Often, when counselors signal the group to line up, only half the group does. Counselors then try various methods to motivate the stragglers to get in line. As they are doing so, those in line become restless and bored and start asking when they are leaving and where they are going, which divides the counselor's attention. The campers in line may then find something to do, such as picking on other campers. If the group has a camper who is a bully, this situation can be very disruptive.

Cues, games, and positive reinforcement can motivate groups to make quick transitions. One idea is for the counselors to have a certain word or phrase that signals campers to clean up their area and line up. Those who do so quickly and quietly will be in the running for leading the group when it moves to the next activity. As the campers clean up and line up, the counselors should point out and praise only the campers who are doing what they are suppose to be doing, and ignore campers who are not following the rules. Once the group is lined up, the counselors pick the leader and instruct the campers to play Follow the Leader as they walk to the next activity. This keeps the children occupied while they are walking.

Transitional times can also be extremely high risk if counselors are not properly supervising or if they have not developed proper routines, strategies, and incentives for campers to make good choices. Two such high-risk times are check-in and checkout because the campers are waiting for others to arrive or waiting to leave. Staff should have activities on hand to occupy campers while they are waiting. Card games, board games, New Games, coloring, building blocks, and Legos are good choices because they are entertaining and easy to supervise.

Other transitional times include locker room times, down time on field trips, the end and start of activities, sunscreen application times, water breaks, the end of lunchtime, and snack time. The staff training should give counselors ideas, resources, and scenarios specific to the age groups they will work with to help them manage transitional times.

Innovative Games

To occupy campers throughout the day, counselors will have to be creative about designing and implementing activities and games. They may decide to use a traditional game as is, modify it to suit the needs of the group, or design a game from scratch. Success depends on the counselor's game design abilities.

Staff trainers should emphasize that children, not games, are most important. Counselors should be taught how to adjust, modify, or alter games to encourage campers to participate and maximize their enjoyment. Additionally, counselors should understand that games are for everyone and that any game can be altered to include a range of interests, abilities, and resources. Figure 6.1 provides a tangible tool for staff to use during the summer season.

Conflict Resolution

Group conflicts, among both campers and counselors, will be the most common occurrence that camp staff will need to mediate throughout the summer. During staff training, offer tips for dealing with conflict in addition to presenting the various types of conflicts that can occur. Conflict resolution should not be about competing with campers or others, accommodating others at the expense of individual needs, or avoidance. Instead, encourage camp staff to employ one of the strategies in figure 6.2 on page 122 when dealing with conflict among campers or one another.

Camp staff must understand that conflicts can be positive and creative and can help campers learn about their own behavior and group dynamics. Staff must also understand how to solve problems peacefully. Give your counselors conflict resolution tools and strategies so that they feel confident heading into the summer season. Also provide opportunities for counselors to improve their skills as part of an ongoing development process.

STRATEGIES FOR DESIGNING GAMES

Three Choices When Designing Games

1. Keep the traditional game as is.
2. Dump the traditional game entirely.
3. Change the traditional game.

Modifying Games

1. Understand the basic structure of games.
2. Change the basic structure of the game.
3. Provide an appropriate degree of difficulty and challenge for the kids.

What Is an Innovative Game?

1. A game designed from scratch
   a. Be creative.
   b. Involve the campers in the evolution of your new game.
   c. Use nontraditional equipment.
2. A traditional game that we modify
   a. Manage the difficulty by using rules, equipment, and game objectives that are developmentally appropriate for your group.
   b. Be flexible in the crafting of modifications.
   c. Use nontraditional equipment.
   d. Five guidelines for modifying games and activities:
      i. Change the size of the equipment.
      ii. Change the size of the playing area.
      iii. Change the skill.
      iv. Change the rules.
      v. Change the instructions.
3. A hybrid activity that we develop (basketball) to be appropriate for our group
   a. Select already established rules that can be used in the hybrid game.
   b. Use a combination of equipment pertinent to the hybrid game.
   c. Be creative with new rules.

Reminders for Game Design

1. Be an enthusiastic leader so that campers are excited about the games!
2. Have fun and celebrate campers' successes!
3. Make sure everyone understands the rules.
4. Reinforce good sporting behavior with shouts of encouragement during the game and boisterous praise afterward.

Figure 6.1 This tool provides strategies for designing games and activities.

5. Maximize participation by not being afraid to modify the game to suit the group's needs.

6. Always be aware of potential and actual safety hazards and minimize injuries.

7. When changing games or transitioning during a game, make sure children understand what is expected so that these changes can take place quickly.

Team Selection

1. Public selection of teams can be humiliating and discourage participation, especially for children typically chosen last or close to last. Instead of letting campers pick teams, pick the teams yourself.

2. When selecting teams, make sure you account for gender equity as well as skill equity, so that females get the same amount of time on the playing arena and those less skilled have ample opportunities to practice and improve.

3. Here are some creative ways to pick teams:
   a. Eye color
   b. Shoe color
   c. Birthday
   d. Alphabetical order
   e. Favorite color
   f. Favorite foods
   g. Numbering off

Figure 6.1 *(continued)*

Ongoing Development

Once the initial staff training week is over, it's time to plan an ongoing staff development program. Your program should include staff meetings, skill refresher trainings, and ongoing verbal reinforcement.

Staff Meetings

Weekly staff meetings are a place to address issues that arise during the week regarding camper behavior, scheduling, or staff morale. However, simply discussing issues without providing tools that your staff can use in their everyday work is a mistake. Consider giving each meeting a topic or theme and provide activities that give your staff a chance to practice skills related to the topic, such as group management, safety, or behavior modification. These types of staff meetings are more meaningful to staff than talking meetings and therefore can boost staff morale and confidence. You might want to incorporate a "kudos" time during meetings in which staff members give peers credit for good work they noticed throughout the week. This can go a long way in boosting morale and confidence even if the meeting agenda consists mostly of areas in need of improvement.

STRATEGIES FOR RESOLVING CONFLICTS

Compromise

- Between assertiveness and cooperation.
- Partial satisfaction of both parties' needs.
- Faster than collaboration but with less exploration of issues.
- Splitting the difference, seeking a quick middle ground.
- Sends the message: *I give up some of the things I want to get other things, and so do you.*

Risk: No one gets all of what they really want. Outcome: Both parties win and lose

Collaboration

- Both assertive and cooperative.
- Alternatives are found to both parties' concerns.
- Both parties explore the issue and identify each other's concerns.
- Sends the message: *We can work together to meet both of our needs fully.*

Risk: It's a lengthy process. Outcome: Win/win

VOEMPing

VOEMPing is a tool to move from conflict to collaboration.

- **V**entilate: Express yourself clearly (*When you _____, I feel _____, because _____.*)
- **O**wnership: Clarify what each party is responsible for; no more, no less.
- **EM**pathize: Articulate how what you did affected the other person.
- **P**lan: Decide how to avoid miscommunications in the future, keeping in mind that mistakes will happen.

Risk: Communication using "I" statements can be easily misinterpreted. Outcome: Campers learn an effective way to express feelings and manage conflict.

Figure 6.2 This tool provides strategies for resolving conflicts.

Adapted, by permission, from University of Vermont Campus Recreation.

Skill Refresher Trainings

Another way to boost staff confidence is to plan time throughout the summer for staff to refresh the skills they learned during certification training or training week. You might also teach new skills you have noticed a need for that you didn't anticipate before camp started. These skill refresher trainings can often be accommodated in a 30-minute period during the staff meeting.

Offer skill refreshers when necessary or, minimally, once or twice during the course of the summer. These types of trainings allow you to honor your commitment to developing your personnel. Skill refresher trainings can include CPR, first aid, or AED scenarios in which counselors are asked to recall the procedures for providing care to campers and then demonstrate those procedures to the group.

Choose topics for refresher trainings based on what you witness during camp. Your counselors may need refreshers in behavior modification, transitional activities, designing games, or working collaboratively with peers. On the off chance that you cannot identify any skills your counselors need to review, consider offering career development trainings on such topics as resume writing, interviewing dos and don'ts, and writing job application letters. These types of trainings honor your commitment to developing your staff in a holistic way.

Verbal Reinforcement and Encouragement

Staff meetings and trainings should not be the only times you provide opportunities for improvement. Plan time to observe your staff and hold short one-on-one meetings to discuss their accomplishments and make suggestions in areas they may need to improve. These meetings are best when scheduled shortly after your observation and during the working day. Putting these meetings off deprives staff members of the opportunity to receive immediate feedback and make immediate adjustments. Short meetings are particularly important for staff members who

Use verbal reinforcement and encouragement during a short one-on-one meeting soon after observing behavior you want to discuss, such as praising a counselor for his easy camaraderie with campers.

need to make changes immediately. Staff members who work well and might need minor changes to become more effective can receive this type of feedback during the formal evaluation process.

Performance Evaluations

The number and scope of staff evaluations depends on the camp. Generally speaking, however, camps should have at least one planned evaluation for all staff members, which may be tough for camps that only offer one or two sessions every summer, but it's worth the effort. Evaluations should be constructive and positive to help staff members grow as professionals beyond their work at camp. During evaluations, help your staff connect the skills they have learned at camp—such as flexibility, communication, and collaboration—to other areas of their personal, professional, and academic lives.

If possible, conduct three staff evaluations during the summer. This gives your staff time to improve their performance while camp is still in session. Staff members need to be aware of their weaknesses and be given tools to address them, as well as given time to use those tools. Providing only one formal evaluation at the end of a camp that lasts longer than six weeks is a disservice to both counselors and campers because it does not give counselors the chance to identify a problem and correct their behavior. Additionally, it allows poor performance to go on without intervention, which directly affects the experience of the campers and can continue to do so.

Specific tools and criteria for staff evaluation vary depending on the camp, but generally, evaluations should provide opportunities for staff to reflect on their work and their feelings about working at camp. Chapter 8 provides specific instruments for evaluating staff performance, and examples and forms are included on the CD-ROM. The three types of staff evaluations are self-evaluations, skill-set evaluations, and ongoing verbal feedback.

Self-evaluations encourage counselors to reflect critically on their work at camp, examining the good work they are doing as well as the areas in which they could improve. This type of evaluation is very meaningful to camp staff, because it allows them to take responsibility for and ownership of their own development.

 Formal skill-set staff evaluations are conducted by the administrative staff (see CD-ROM form 6.11: Counselor Final Camp Evaluation). You may choose to read counselors' self-evaluations before writing your skill-set evaluations because the work of some counselors may have gone unnoticed throughout the summer.

The final and most informal type of evaluation at camp is ongoing verbal feedback. This is good for developing, motivating, and training the staff throughout the summer season and was discussed earlier in this section.

Counselor-in-Training Programs

A final staffing consideration is whether to incorporate a counselor-in-training (CIT) program. CIT programs typically identify community teenagers who are interested in learning about becoming counselors but may not be ready for the full responsibility. CIT programs have an application process and generally a cost for participating, which is received by the camp in the same manner as camper registration. However, not all CIT programs have costs associated with them. The decision of whether to charge CITs for participation should be informed by community expectations, the cost of running the CIT program, and the overall camp budget.

Most CIT programs combine hands-on experience working with camper groups with education in child development, learning styles, game design, and behavior modification. Use the staff training week outline and break the topics down to provide more specific examples, scenarios, and development opportunities for CITs. CIT training should happen the weekend after counselor training but before the start of camp and can take place in one day. Typically the training will include learning outcomes in the areas identified above coupled with practice time to apply the skills learned during training. It can range from four to six hours, depending on the size of the group and the level of participation of the hired counselors. After bonding for a week, counselors can be a huge asset to the administrative staff in getting CITs on board and having the counselors they will be working with take responsibility for portions of the training. Finally, the program should be well rounded and provide time for CITs to hang out informally with each other to develop a peer community, which is very important to teenagers. Planning formal activities for the CIT program may be warranted to justify any fee associated with the program. These may include field trips off site for fun and relaxation away from camp.

CIT programs are valuable to camps, but they also create some challenges. Teenagers are still developing physically, emotionally, and cognitively. This means that their judgment may not be very good, they may lack a good work ethic, and they may lack the motivation to fully participate. Depending on them as counselor helpers may be problematic. Also, at times CITs can behave worse than campers. For example, sometimes CITs have a hard time seeing themselves in the role of counselor. They may be more concerned with creating fun for campers during the

Counselor-in-training programs give community teenagers hands-on experience working with campers.

games, favor some campers over others, and pay little attention to the instructions of the counselor staff or the rules of the group.

To counteract these issues, develop a CIT program that clearly defines the program and the role of CITs. Stipulations of what CITs can and cannot do when working with children should be communicated to the CITs and staff as part of the training for each group. Training CITs prior to their arrival may be necessary, but this can usually be accommodated in a few hours rather than a day or several days. A CIT program is a good service to the community and can help the camp meet staffing needs if the budget is tight, but it must be planned thoroughly and implemented effectively to maximize the benefits to the camp, the camp staff, and the individual CITs.

Conclusion

Staffing your camp well is the most important thing you can do to reach camp goals and advance the camp mission to provide a high-quality experience for community youth while keeping campers safe. Staffing considerations include establishing minimal qualifications, developing hiring procedures, creating a staff training program, offering ongoing staff development, addressing staff accountability and evaluations, and developing CIT programs.

From Rogue CIT to All-Star Counselor

While I was working at a facility-based day camp in New England, I wanted to extend our reach to teenagers in the area, so I introduced a CIT program to engage community youth over the age of 14 (which was the ending age of the camp). I began the process of planning the program; marketing to my constituency; making contacts with the local high schools; and developing the requirements, protocols, and expectations of the individuals who would be filling the CIT roles. Before long I had several applications from interested teens and chose what I hoped would be good candidates for the first class of the new CIT program.

For the first few weeks, all of the CITs were engaged and happy in the process, and the counselors seemed to be satisfied with their level of performance. However, I was blissfully unaware of the behavior of one CIT who was disrupting the counselors' plans. To their credit, the counselors tried to address the issue themselves, but after two weeks, they brought it to my attention. They explained how the CIT played games too roughly with the campers; did not adjust his skills to suit the campers' level; became irate when rules were interpreted by the counselors in an unfavorable light; rallied campers against counselors; favored some campers over others; and did not listen to the counselors when it was time to move on, clean up, or stop.

I called the CIT into my office for a conversation in which I identified the areas for improvement in his behavior. He offered many excuses—expectations were not clear, counselors treated him unfairly, and so on. I reviewed with him the constructs of the program, his contract, and the CIT training topics, and I gave him conflict resolution strategies for dealing with situations in which he felt the counselors were wrong. I also encouraged him to talk to me as needed. He seemed receptive to the ideas and began visiting me every day for about a week. At our meetings, I continued to offer strategies and encouragement.

Over the next few weeks, he came to me less often, so I asked his counselors how he was doing. They reported that he had become a different CIT: He was more thoughtful in his interactions with counselors, listened better, stopped playing rough, was more creative in getting campers' attention, and incorporated strategies that they had learned in training. The rest of the summer went smoothly, and the CIT continued to grow and even outshone some of his peers.

At the end of the summer, the CIT wrote in his reflections that he had been bored and distracted at the beginning of the program, perhaps because he felt that his parents had forced him to be there. After my intervention, he felt valued from being considered mature enough to deal with the issues and being viewed as a peer by the counselors in his group. He gained confidence from the trust the camp placed in him by giving him concrete skills. As a result of reading his journal, I made our CIT program much more intentional in subsequent years. As for the CIT, he came back as a counselor the next two years, winning the Counselor of the Summer award in his second year as a full-time staff member. The CIT program worked for the logistical needs of the camp, developed him holistically, and inspired me to make the expectations of our CITs higher, more concrete, and more intentional.

Minimal staff qualifications include a genuine desire to work with children, experience working with children, and minimal certification. Other aspects of the hiring process include recruitment, the application process, the interview process, and background checks and other paperwork. In addition to running a staff training week, you will also want to develop your staff throughout the summer through weekly staff meetings, refresher trainings, and ongoing feedback. Finally, staff accountability and evaluations are important, as is the consideration of a CIT program. In the next chapter, camp programming will be described as the next stage in developing a camp program or revitalizing an existing program.

Programming the Camp

The first step in developing day camp programs and activities that will be well received by the community is to examine programming trends in facility-based camps across the country. Although the specifics of your camp will depend on the community you serve, using the experience of established camp programs will help you solidify your camp schedule (see CD-ROM form 7.1: Camp Daily Schedule), provide innovative programming, and offer a high-quality camp experience. Understanding basic program design issues and concerns will help you gauge whether programs that are popular in other parts of the country are going to be feasible at your camp. This chapter outlines a variety of programs and describes how to select the ones best suited to your camp and how to implement them.

FORM 7.1

Camp Daily Schedule

Group 1, Session 1

	Monday (6/22)	Tuesday (6/23)	Wednesday (6/24)	Thursday (6/25)	Friday (6/26)
8:00-8:30	8:00-8:15 Check-in	Check-in	Check-in	8:00-8:30 Check-in	Check-in
	8:15-8:30 All-camp meeting			8:30-9:10 Arts and crafts	
8:30-9:30	Arts and crafts	Arts and crafts	Arts and crafts	9:10-9:30 Prep for departure	Arts and crafts
9:30-9:45	Morning snack	Morning snack	Morning snack	9:30 Buses leave for Echo	Morning snack
9:45-10:30	Kids and fitness	Kids and fitness	Kids and fitness	10:00-12:00 Explore Echo	Kids and fitness
10:30-11:00	Change	Change	Change	12:00-12:25 Lunch at waterfront	Change
11:00-12:00	Aquatics	Aquatics	Aquatics	12:25-12:50 Games at waterfront	Aquatics
12:00-12:30	Change	Change	Change	12:50-1:00 Prep for departure	Change
12:30-12:55	Lunch	Lunch	Lunch	1:00 Buses leave Echo	Lunch
12:55-1:15	Break	Break	Break	1:30-2:00 Group choice	Break
1:15-1:30	Team building	Team building	Team building	2:00-2:45 Sports and games	Team building
1:30-2:00	Group choice	Group choice	Group choice	2:45-3:05 Change	Group choice
2:00-2:45	Sports and games	Sports and games	Sports and games	3:05-3:55 Free swim	Sports and games
2:45-4:15	2:45-3:05 Change	2:45-3:30 Club 1	2:45-3:30 Club 1	3:55-4:15 Change	All-camp activity
	3:05-3:55 Free swim	3:30-4:15 Club 2	3:30-4:15 Club 2	4:15-4:30 Afternoon snack	Field day!
	3:55-4:15 Change			4:30-5:00 Checkout	
4:15-4:30	Afternoon snack	Afternoon snack	Afternoon snack		Afternoon snack
4:30-5:00	Checkout	Checkout	Checkout		Checkout

From J. Moffitt, 2011, *Day camp programming and administration: Core skills and practices* (Champaign, IL: Human Kinetics). Adapted, by permission, from University of Vermont Campus Recreation.

During the initial days of camp, try not to get bogged down in thinking about every possible thing that could go wrong with programming and schedules. You will undoubtedly face a plethora of items that need to be changed or that didn't go smoothly. That is fine. The most important thing to remember is to be flexible and patient. This is especially true in the first week of camp, and most especially on the first day. Now that all of the plans for the camp have been made and the staff has been trained, your job is to be accessible to staff, campers, and parents and guardians when needed.

CAMP STORIES

Being Available

Early in my career, I did not understand what it meant to "be available" as a camp administrator because I had not yet learned how important being visible among staff, campers, and parents was to the long-term success of the camp program. I can recall thinking, in my first year as an administrator working at a camp in the Midwest, that all I had to do was plan the programs, hire the staff, and sit back in my office and watch it all take off. Which I did for about two days, until the camp had a major accident that I had to deal with, and I realized that I didn't remember the counselor's name, much less the child's, and now I had to call the parents. It was a great early lesson for me because I made so many mistakes in that first round. In addition to not knowing names, I didn't know the schedule (I planned it but did not memorize it) for any of the groups; I didn't know which kids belonged to which parents; and I didn't know how poorly my staff was implementing and planning games because they had absolutely no help, feedback, or guidance from me. As a result, a severe accident happened, and I had to scramble to find out what I needed to know to handle the situation with some level of intelligence and competence, despite my lack of attention to these meaningful details. After that, I decided to make an intentional effort to get out more, learn the counselors' names, learn the campers' names, and meet parents. As I began to do that, I was able to identify the areas in which the staff needed help, play games with campers, and develop more meaningful relationships with the staff I wanted to develop and campers that were becoming part of my community. Additionally, I had a lot more fun engaging in this way than sitting back, watching, and waiting. The outcomes of my actions were that staff games got better and became safer and relationships with campers and parents became stronger. This was a major asset when another accident occurred later in the summer to the child of a family that I had developed a relationship with. The difference between my reaction and the parental reaction of the first and second incidents that summer were night and day, and both of the reactions were indicative of my level of availability to do the right things. It was about being committed to the goals of my organization and honoring the plan fully by being present, engaged, and invested in the welfare of the community I wanted to create.

Being in touch with your staff during camp is essential for helping them succeed. Get out and learn campers' names, join programs on occasion, observe and guide counselors toward autonomy, and generally make yourself available. Camp administrators who sit behind closed doors all day struggle reaching goals, fail at maintaining high staff morale, and look foolish when speaking to parents and guardians about children whose names they did not bother to learn.

Common Programs

This section describes 20 common programs you can easily modify for your camp. The descriptions come from personal experience, a review of the current literature, and program evaluations examined for this book. They are not derived from one source, but are a compilation of programs across the United States. The programs described here are the most popular and affordable for facility-based camps. It is important to remember that, although any program can be factored into the cost of camp (what families pay), expensive programs may not be reasonable for certain communities.

Arts and Crafts

Arts and crafts programs address spatial, creative, and cognitive skills for all stages of development. A dedicated, experienced, and creative instructor is the key to an arts and crafts program's success. It requires a room that can accommodate a number of campers and an investment in arts and crafts supplies. (See CD-ROM form 7.2: Arts and Crafts Program Goals, Objectives, and Standards.)

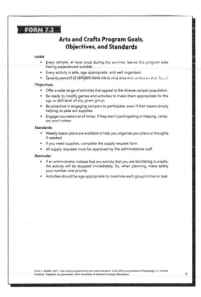

All-Camp Programs

All-camp programs engage the entire camp in an activity regardless of age. The purpose is to mix age groups so that campers have a chance to meet other campers who are not in their daily groups. Popular activities include scavenger hunts, counselor hunts (campers have to find counselors hiding around camp while staying together as a group), and relay races. All-camp programs are very inexpensive and can use any space as long as it is large enough to accommodate the number of campers participating. The key to this program is to develop activities that appeal to all age groups and to mix the age groups fairly.

Performance Arts

Performance arts programs combine elements of music, drama, and dance and emphasize creativity and exploration. The key to the success of a performance arts program is an interested, passionate, and excited leader who can design a program that allows kids to choose the element of performance they want to try. Equipment costs can be high for this program because costumes, stages, set design, and makeup might be required, depending on the goals of the camp. If your camp takes place on a college campus, consider using the resources of the music, theater, and dance departments. These departments are often willing to provide some equipment, help design the program, or provide the space for a small donation or free of charge for the sake of sharing their knowledge with the next generation. If you do not have access to such departments, simply find an area large enough so that children can express themselves in movement and with starter instruments.

The key to a successful performance arts program is an interested, passionate, and excited leader.

Innovative Games

Innovative games are sometimes referred to as New Games. They emphasize fun and movement, encouraging children to move naturally in a noncompetitive environment. Innovative games require large places to play and often use nontraditional, inexpensive equipment such as hula hoops, jump ropes, scooters, and board walkers.

Fitness Fun

You can combat the obesity epidemic head-on in your community by providing a camper fitness program. If you have access to the larger organization's fitness equipment, the cost can be minimal. Kids love medicine balls, kickboxing gloves, jump ropes, mini-trampolines, and step boards, so why not incorporate these into your camp program? To do so, you need space, equipment, and a qualified instructor. (See CD-ROM form 7.3: Camp Fitness Program Goals, Objectives, and Standards.)

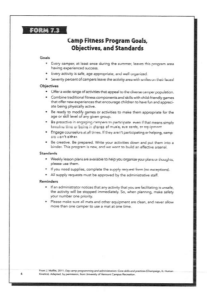

Nature

Organizations with access to natural areas will get the most out of nature programs. Nevertheless, a classroom can be used as a learning place when natural areas or greenhouses are not available. Simple walks to look for birds, insects, and leaves are always popular among campers. Nature programs require minimal equipment, are easily modified for most settings, and require a qualified instructor to make the most of the camp's surroundings and resources. Geology, natural resources, and environmental science departments may be willing to help campus recreation providers design and implement nature programs. (See CD-ROM form 7.4: Naturally Fun Program Goals, Objectives, and Standards.)

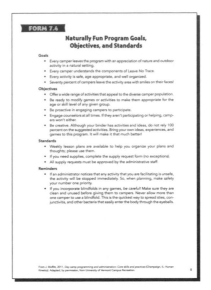

Informal Play

Every camp program needs a time during the day when kids just play with no direction from adults. A large field with varied equipment or a playground area is ideal for informal play, which should be short and well supervised. Counselors should not interact with campers while they are playing. Their number one responsibility is to supervise and troubleshoot, not to design and implement games.

Team Building

Team-building programs emphasize teamwork, cooperative learning, and problem solving through short activities that stress communication and respect. Hundreds of web sites offer team-building, ice-breaking, and other cooperative learning activities and publications that require no additional or special equipment, and in most cases, no equipment at all. Team building can be done in a room, hallway, field, or gym depending on the size of the group.

Clubs

Clubs offer a great deal of variety and flexibility to both staff and campers. Camps providing clubs generally offer campers six or seven activities to choose from during the day. Activities can include anything from traditional sports, outdoor recreation, leisure activities, and the performance arts to water games and classic games. Limit club times to 45 minutes, and allow campers to vary their choices from day to day. Because some clubs are more popular than others, you will have to limit the number of campers that can be in clubs at any one time. Clubs can cost very little, and in many cases nothing, because camp equipment can be used during club time. Campers benefit from opportunities to participate in their favorite activities or try something completely different.

Team-building activities are designed to develop team communication and respect.

Wall Climbing

Universities and colleges that have climbing walls should maximize their use! If you have access to a climbing wall, expect to pay to certify your staff to safely work the wall and for smaller harnesses for your campers. A climbing program is a great way for kids to spend their camp day for a limited cost and maximum fun. (See CD-ROM form 7.5: Climbing Release of Liability.)

FORM 7.5

Climbing Release of Liability

Release and Indemnification of All Claims and Covenant Not to Sue

Notice: This is a legally binding agreement. By signing this agreement, you give up your right to bring a court action to recover compensation or obtain any other remedy for any injury to yourself or your property or for your death, however caused, arising from your use of the vertical climbing wall, now or any time in the future.

Acknowledgment of Risk

I, _____ hereby acknowledge and agree that the sport of indoor rock climbing and the use of the vertical climbing wall (hereinafter referred to as the climbing wall) located in the _____ has inherent risks. I have full knowledge of the nature and extent of all risks associated with indoor rock climbing and the use of the climbing wall, including but not limited to the following:

1. All manner of injury resulting from falling off the climbing wall and impacting the wall surface and projections (handholds, railings, other climbers, belaying hardware) or the facility floor.
2. Rope abrasions, entanglement, and other injuries resulting from activities on or near the climbing wall such as, but not limited to, climbing, belaying, rappelling, lowering, or using any rescue systems or rope techniques.
3. Injuries resulting from falling climbers or dropped items, such as, but not limited to, ropes, climbing hardware, holds, and tools.
4. Cuts from abrasions resulting from skin contact with the climbing wall.
5. Failure of ropes, slings, harnesses, climbing hardware, anchor points, or any part of the climbing wall structure.

I further acknowledge that the preceding list is not exclusive of all possible risks associated with the use of the climbing wall and that the list in no way limits the extent or reach of this release and covenant not to sue.

Climber's signature _____

Date _____

Parent's or guardian's signature
(if climber is under 18 years old) _____

Date _____

From J. Moffitt, 2011, *Day camp programming and administration: Core skills and practices* (Champaign, IL: Human Kinetics). Adapted, by permission, from University of Vermont Campus Recreation.

Outdoor or Adventure Recreation

Outdoor recreation programs can be designed around your facilities or in outdoor areas on campus or in your local community. They are versatile, flexible, and, when designed properly, fun. As with any program, the key is to hire a dedicated, knowledgeable, and creative person to provide outdoor recreation opportunities that use the campus and surrounding community resources to the fullest. Although the cost of a good outdoor recreation program will be substantial, an experienced instructor can help you modify the cost. Programs include hiking, walking, kayaking, canoeing, biking, indoor or outdoor rock climbing, ropes course activities, and camping. (See CD-ROM form 7.6: Ropes Course Liability and Medical Information.)

Special Events

Special events offer campers and staff a refreshing change in the daily schedule. They include magicians, camp talent shows, ice cream parties, "dive-in" movies (i.e., watching a movie that is projected on the wall while campers are on rafts and floats in the pool), traveling theater performances, college and university athlete exposition shows, college and university mascot visits, and inflatable obstacle courses and moon walks. These types of events are especially good for camps at institutions with strict policies against traveling with minors as well as for camps that serve children whose parents and guardians are apprehensive about putting them on buses to go on field trips. Special events can be accommodated on several sport courts, open gyms, or open fields. Expect to spend anywhere from $50 to $500 for a special event, depending on the event.

Sports

Traditional sports that day camps offer include basketball, baseball, football, soccer, field hockey, ice hockey, and tennis. To offer these, you will need a gym,

Many traditional sports offer special recreational camps, which focus more on participation and fun than developing skills.

fields, and multipurpose courts. The focus of recreational day camp sport programs (in contrast to specialty sport camps) should be maximum participation and fun, not skill acquisition. You may already have access to sport equipment in your organization, but if you need to buy new equipment, make sure it is kid friendly, durable, and inexpensive.

Horseback Riding

Horseback riding lessons depend on the opportunities that exist in the community. If your camp is located on a campus that has a stable or equestrian team, you may be able to negotiate with stable managers to use the horses and programs. If you do not have access to a stable, you may seek out resources in your community. Anytime a program is located off site, the cost will be substantial because of risk, liability, and transportation issues. However, these costs can be offset by passing them on to campers or by bartering with the providers.

Start early (i.e., October) negotiating these opportunities with local providers. You may be surprised to learn that many providers care deeply about promoting the activity and are willing to provide programs at cost. Also, emphasize the opportunity you are offering to spread the word about their programs. Campers who like the camp lessons may sign up for lessons at the stables throughout the year.

Aquatics

Aquatics encompasses a variety of pool-based (as opposed to waterfront) activities that are generally easy and inexpensive to implement if you have access to a pool. Programs include water fitness, swim lessons, and free swim (see CD-ROM form 7.7: Camper Swim Test Log). All aquatic activities require a certified lifeguard, and swim lessons require certified water safety instructors who can teach campers of all ages and ability levels. You may decide to hire an aquatic staff with experience in these activities to supplement the other camp programs or to spend several hours training your regular camp counselors (prior to the start of camp) to provide aquatic lessons. This decision will depend on your larger organization's aquatic policies and regulations as well as your program's budget (see CD-ROM form 7.8: Aquatic Program Goals, Objectives, and Standards).

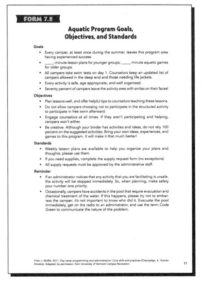

Waterfront

Waterfront activities, such as skiing, paddle boating, kayaking, and canoeing, differ from aquatic activities in that they require extensive bodies of water. If your camp does not have a waterfront area, consider offering waterfront activities to campers once or twice during the summer. (See CD-ROM form 7.9: Boating Release of Liability.)

The cost of waterfront activities (including equipment maintenance for camps owning equipment) should be incorporated into the cost of the camp. Some communities are able to pay the increased fees for waterfront programs. If you are serving a lower-income community, try to negotiate trades with local providers to offset the costs of the program.

FORM 7.9

Boating Release of Liability

Program name _____ Date _____

Participant name _____

Address _____

Phone(s) (___) ___-_____   (___) ___-_____

In case of emergency, please notify _____ at

_____

Alternate emergency contact _____ at

Outfitting information:

Age _____ Height _____ Weight _____ Gender _____

What is your child's swimming ability or comfort level in the water?

_____

_____

What are your and your child's expectations for this program?

_____

_____

Does your child have any medical, physical, or emotional conditions that might
affect our teaching methods or your child's experience? Please describe them.

_____

Does your child take any medications? Please list them. If your child uses an inhaler
for asthma, does he or she carry it at all times? How often does your child use it
under normal circumstances? If your child has diabetes, what is his or her treatment
regimen?

_____

Does your child have any allergies? If allergic to bees, does your child carry a bee
sting kit?

_____

_____

From J. Moffitt, 2011, *Day camp programming and administration: Core skills and practices* (Champaign, IL: Human Kinetics). Adapted, by permission, from University of Vermont Campus Recreation.

12

Ice Activities

If you have access to an on-site ice rink, you can offer ice activities. Even if you can schedule ice time only once or twice during a session, take advantage of those opportunities by providing lessons, organizing broomball games, or holding open skates (campers will most likely have to bring their own skates, and this should be communicated to parents and guardians in advance). If you are seeking ice time off site, plan to spend a great deal of money. Ultimately, your decision to offer an ice program will depend on the community you serve and your financial resources.

Archery

Archery is an easy program to implement in any recreational day camp. Many physical education departments on college campuses already have adequate equipment for a solid archery program. Collaborating with a physical education department to use its equipment (a trade or small rental fee may need to be negotiated) and hiring qualified instructors are an easy route to designing a program that safely introduces this nontraditional sport to campers. Use a large indoor multipurpose space; a long, wide hallway; or a field for your archery program. Communicate safety rules adequately to all campers and staff, and enforce the rules at all times during the program.

Laser Tag

Laser tag is best accommodated off site at a professional range. Although campers love this activity, it is not necessarily cost effective. Even though you may be able to negotiate a group rate, the cost of transporting campers to a range can be high. Laser tag can be offered daily or weekly depending on your budget,

Safety is an important consideration when offering an archery program.

although it may not be cost effective for extremely large camps that require several buses. However, it may be appropriate for smaller camps to offer once or twice throughout the summer. Finding a provider that is trustworthy and safe and collecting participation waivers from campers' parents and guardians are imperative.

Field Trips

Field trips at recreational day camps can be either on site or off site. On-site trips may be more appealing and appropriate for certain age groups or certain communities and can include walks to campus museums, planetariums, farms or stables, or greenhouses. These are good programs for younger kids if parents and guardians are apprehensive about bus travel, particularly for children under the age of eight. They are also less expensive than off-site trips. Off-site field trips are popular among campers and staff because they offer a break from the

regular schedule (see CD-ROM form 7.10: Camp Field Trip Schedule) and provide opportunities for campers to see and get to know the community they live in. Field trips are expensive but worth the expense because they tend to be programs campers remember best and look forward to year after year.

Camp Field Trip Schedule

Field Trip (Thursday)

Group 1	Group 2	Group 3
8:00-8:30 Check-in	8:00-8:30 Check-in	8:00-8:30 Check-in
8:30-9:10 Arts and crafts	8:30-9:15 Sports and games	8:30-8:50 Change
9:10-9:30 Prep for departure	9:15-9:30 Morning snack	8:50-9:50 Aquatics
9:30 Buses leave for Echo	9:30-10:00 Prep for departure	9:50-10:10 Change
10:00-12:00 Explore Echo	10:00 Buses leave for Echo	10:10-10:30 Prep for departure
12:00-12:25 Lunch at waterfront	10:30-10:50 Games at waterfront	10:30 Buses leave for Echo
12:25-12:50 Games at waterfront	10:50-12:50 Explore Echo	11:00-11:30 Lunch at waterfront
12:50-1:00 Prep for departure	12:50-1:15 Lunch	11:30-12:00 Games at waterfront
1:00 Buses leave Echo	1:15-1:30 Prep for departure	12:00-1:45 Explore Echo
1:30-2:00 Group choice	1:30 Buses leave Echo	1:45 Prep for departure
2:00-2:45 Sports and games	2:00-2:45 Kids and fitness	2:00 Buses leave Echo
2:45-3:05 Change	2:45-3:45 Arts and crafts	2:30-3:00 Group choice
3:05-3:55 Free swim	3:45-4:00 Afternoon snack	3:00-3:35 Kids and fitness
3:55-4:15 Change	4:00-4:30 Group choice	3:35-3:50 Afternoon snack
4:15-4:30 Afternoon snack	4:30-5:00 Checkout	3:50-4:30 Arts and crafts
4:30-5:00 Checkout		4:30-5:00 Checkout

CAMP COUNSEL

Inclusive Programming at Facility-Based Day Camps

Every facility-based day camp should provide for campers with disabilities. Although there is no one way to include campers with special needs or disabilities, some essential attitudes and philosophies among the camp staff will make the inclusion of all campers, regardless of ability, a priority. Encourage your staff to do the following:

- Have a positive attitude about including all campers. Do not act like making the group or game a welcoming space is a chore.
- Have clear and consistent expectations for all campers.
- Remember that everybody counts.
- Consider adaptations for those that need them.
- Treat all children equally, but not the same.

In addition to the preceding, give your staff the following strategies for including campers with disabilities or special needs:

- Make sure your activity takes place in a space or location that is accessible to everyone.
- Use campers. Encourage camper pairing so that a child with a disability has someone to work with.
- Make sure that everyone gets to participate in all activities.
- Ask parents and guardians about the specific disabilities and needs of their child and discuss how to accommodate the child's needs.
- When working around a table, leave a space without a chair to accommodate a person who uses a wheelchair.
- Keep all pathways free of clutter.
- Place all supplies and equipment within reach of everyone.

Program Selection and Implementation

When selecting programs, consider the design of the activities and how they will affect the daily schedule of all groups the camp serves. Other considerations include program trends, your resource inventory, and your community needs assessment. Program selection can be difficult when you have to consider the needs of the larger organization at which the camp is housed.

Use the physical and human resources at your disposal to smooth program implementation. This will require an enormous amount of open, honest communication with all stakeholders and organizational leaders. Also very important is planning activities in advance.

Your staff will greatly benefit from using activity lesson plans (see CD-ROM form 7.11: Activity Lesson Plans) and requests for supplies (see CD-ROM form 7.12: Request for Supplies) when designing play time, games, and activities for campers. These encourage staff to be forward thinking and prepared. If having all counselors create lesson plans and request supplies is not practical, encourage at least the program activity leaders to do so.

Conclusion

The 20 programs outlined in this chapter were selected because they can easily be incorporated into or modified for most facility-based day camps. This list is not intended to be all inclusive but simply to provide the basic building blocks for camp programming. Revisiting your initial needs assessment, financial plan, and human resources inventory can help you select programs that will be well received by your community. The final chapter discusses how to evaluate your camp's programming and administrative components.

Evaluating the Camp

Evaluation is an important step in the camp process, yet so many organizations do not put in the effort required to evaluate their camps appropriately. With that said, it is helpful to keep in mind that there is no single way to evaluate a camp program. Moreover, you are guaranteed to make mistakes when instituting an evaluation plan for the first time. These mistakes can be managed, however, and meaningful data can still be garnered even if the evaluations are flawed. Also, if you surveyed the community during the camp development phase, you may find aspects of creating an evaluation process familiar, because the two processes are similar. The point is to go through the process and to learn from it so that your evaluations improve and help the camp to evolve.

This chapter addresses the need for camp evaluations and highlights examples of evaluations. The chapter briefly reviews the distribution of evaluations without much detail because survey distribution (which is similar) was discussed fully in chapter 2. Next, the chapter provides an overview of two evaluation tools to complete during camp as a course of best practice. The chapter concludes with a discussion of ways to analyze the evaluation data to inform decisions that will ensure the stability of the camp.

Evaluating Programs

Program evaluations that provide the most well-rounded feedback use multiple data discovery and analysis processes that address the top three stakeholders of any camp: staff, parents and guardians, and campers. However, few facility-based camps have the time or financial resources to implement multiple strategies. If you are in this situation, focus on getting feedback from your largest or most important stakeholders, which in most cases are parents and guardians.

Staff Feedback

Feedback from staff will help you measure the success of the processes, plans, and protocols of the camp. The authentic voice of the frontline workers (counselors and other staff) is essential for ascertaining what really happens at the camp. You may perceive that all is well, but the staff knows the whole story and, in some cases, the true story. Addressing the concerns, issues, and needs of staff every year is good business practice and helps ensure staff retention.

One way to get feedback from your staff is to ask them to complete and submit a quick survey with questions about their perceptions of the organization, planning, and implementation of camp programs. Make sure the survey questions are not unintentionally leading and that they are easy to read and understand (see CD-ROM form 8.1: Staff Evaluation of Camp). Consider using a Likert scale, in which participants are asked to specify their level of agreement to a statement. Table 8.1 shows examples of language and scales used in Likert scaled instruments and questionnaires.

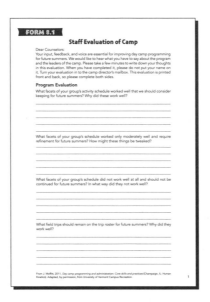

Likert Scale

Because Likert scales are common, your staff will be familiar with using them. And because they are easy to develop, you can focus on the types of questions to ask, how to ask them, and how they will fall on the scale. Although every camp program will have unique requirements for its surveys, there are some commonalities. Bob Algozzine offers some good tips for creating a Likert scale, which are summarized here.

- Use statements that refer to the present rather than the past (e.g., *I think the registration process is efficient* vs. *I thought the registration process was efficient*).
- Avoid statements that are factual or could be interpreted as factual (e.g., instead of *The camper discipline policy is a strong policy that effectively modifies behavior*, use *I believe the camper discipline policy is an effective tool to help modify behavior*).

- Avoid irrelevant statements. If you want to know how parents and guardians feel about the registration process, do not address anything outside the registration process. For example, the statement *I wish the registration process would accept the Discover Card as a method of payment* is about payment, not registration.

- Avoid general statements that just about everyone (or no one) is likely to endorse (e.g., *Camp met my full expectations every day*).

- Use statements that cover the entire range of the affective scale (e.g., *The camp met my expectations*).

- Use statements that are simple, clear, and direct.

- Make statements short (e.g., not exceeding 20 words).

- Use only one complete thought in each statement to ensure that they are not interpreted in more than one way. For example, the statement *I found the camp program to be well organized and fun* includes two thoughts. The program can be organized and not fun, or fun but not organized. In clumping these thoughts together in this statement, the survey requires that the respondent choose which one was more important—fun or organization. During data analysis, you will not be able to tell which area needs work.

- Avoid universal words such as *all, always, none,* and *never,* because they may introduce ambiguity.

Table 8.1 Likert Scale Example Language and Assigned Values

Type of scale	POINTS ON CONTINUUM				
	1	2	3	4	5
Agreement	Strongly agree	Agree	Neither agree nor disagree	Disagree	Strongly disagree
Frequency	Always	Often	About half the time	Seldom	Never
Satisfaction	Very satisfied	Satisfied	Neither satisfied nor dissatisfied	Dissatisfied	Very dissatisfied
Effectiveness	Very effective	Effective	Neither effective nor ineffective	Ineffective	Very ineffective
Quality	Very good	Good	Average	Poor	Very poor
Expectancy	Much better than expected	Better than expected	As expected	Worse than expected	Much worse than expected
Extent	To a very great extent	To a great extent	Somewhat	To a small extent	To a very small extent

Table designed by Bob Algozzine (Likert, 1932; Pershing, 2000).

Reprinted, by permission, from B. Algozzine. Available http://education.uncc.edu/rfalgozz/ADMN8699/likerttips.pdf

- Use words such as *only, just, merely,* and so on with care and in moderation because they can lead the respondent.

- Whenever possible, use simple sentences rather than compound or complex sentences.

- Avoid the use of words that respondents may not understand. Technical terms should be explained, and acronyms should be avoided altogether.

- Avoid the use of double negatives (e.g., *I don't think the camp shouldn't change anything*).

Adapted, by permission, from B. Algozzine. Available http://education.uncc.edu/rfalgozz/ADMN8699/likerttips.pdf

A Likert scale questionnaire or other evaluation tool is good, but it may not give your staff enough of an opportunity to discuss important issues that you may not have considered when you drew up the questions. A focus group may give you more meaningful data that you can compare with parent and camper feedback.

Focus Group

A focus group is a gathering of staff for about one hour to share reflections of the camp. The last staff meeting of the season may be a good time to do this. Whenever you schedule it, be sure to choose a time and place that maximizes participation. Small focus groups work best (but not too small; you should have at least four participants). Depending on the size of your staff, you may need to divide the focus group into smaller groups of five to eight people that take place at the same time.

Focus group questions should be focused, specific, and clear. Focus groups are not problem-solving sessions; rather, they are more like interviews. Questions should invite dialogue so that participants can hear from their peers and feed off their responses. Ask specific questions about staff issues that you want feedback on, such as, *How effective do you think staff training was?* You can then follow this lead-in interview question with one asking participants to identify what changes, specifically, they believe need to be made.

If you are holding several focus groups simultaneously, keep them as similar as possible. One way to do this is to script the questions. Additionally, brief facilitators on the point of a focus group and remind them that their role is to ask, observe, and record, not to judge staff or become defensive. Under no circumstances are facilitators to respond to participants' answers unless they invoke follow-up questions. Focus groups are intended to be fluid; however, camps implementing this method for the first time should stick to the script. Follow-up questions are best used only by experienced facilitators who are comfortable with the ambiguity of the process and the unpredictability of participants.

Facilitators will also need to be trained on documenting the feedback consistently. Determine whether answers will be recorded on paper or through sound recorders. Facilitators should refrain from offering personal insights into the meaning of participants' responses in their documentation. Again, their role is to ask, record, and observe; your role is to analyze what they have recorded. To do so, you will need data that are as unbiased as possible.

Focus group questions should be developed with a general purpose and a specific intention in mind. In other words, identify what the purpose of the questions will be on a general level, such as to solicit feedback on camp policies. Then develop

A focus group gives staff members the chance to reflect back on the camp. Small groups discuss specific questions, which, for example, could address how well received the new pool basketball program was.

questions around the various policies employed at camp, such as the refund policy, payment policies, discipline policy, and dress code, which are questions intended to examine specific camp policies. Follow these guidelines:

- Determine the most important things you want to know from staff.
- Develop simple, but general, questions that address the issues you want to know about.
- Create questions that address the three most important issues.

For example, if your goal is to find out whether staff members felt adequately supported by the administration, you might phrase the question this way: *What barriers have you encountered in terms of getting the support you wanted or needed to be successful at camp?* If your goal is to find out whether the staff found the daily schedule effective, you might ask, *What changes in the daily schedule would you like to see?*

In addition, the amount of time you set aside for the focus group will determine the number of questions you use. Focus groups scheduled for less than an hour will go quickly, so one to three questions is appropriate for this length of time. One hour is sufficient for smaller groups of six to eight participants. If the groups are smaller than this, don't be afraid to make adjustments to the time or number of questions.

Abiding by general guidelines is good practice. In general, focus groups should not address more than six questions, should not be larger than 15 participants, and should not last longer than 60 minutes. In the end, however, the information you obtain and how you use that information are what is most important.

Finally, keep in mind that focus group participants can be swayed by what others in the group say. Because focus groups are dialogues, participants may change their views during the course of the conversation. Facilitators should note and record participants' dialogues and changes of opinion. These notes will help you make decisions about camp changes and are an important part of the focus group process.

Although a focus group may not be as objective as you would like, when determining what is best for a camp and its community, qualitative information is more important than quantitative information. Focus groups often provide deeper and richer contexts than surveys do, which can result in a more critical and thoughtful analysis on your part when determining what changes to make to the program.

Parent and Guardian Feedback

For most camps, the easiest way to collect large quantities of feedback is with an evaluation tool in the form of a survey or questionnaire. Additionally, to get the most participation and the most varied feedback from a large constituency such as parents and guardians, you will need a quick, nonevasive, and efficient evaluation tool. Focus groups are less practical for this group. Distributing this type of evaluation is discussed later in this chapter; this section addresses developing the tool.

The nature of the camp will dictate what items the parent evaluation should include. It should be specific to the camp and the community and should be user friendly and easy to follow. A Likert scale is useful for this large and varied group. Because you will not get to ask everything you want to, prioritize your questions and include only those you deem most important. (See CD-ROM form 8.2: Parent and Guardian Evaluation of Camp.)

Generally speaking, a parent evaluation should address child safety, child fun, the daily schedule, discipline policies, communication policies, and the level of care provided by staff. Many programs want feedback on camp operational structures and procedures such as registration, fees, policies, and parents' and guardians' overall satisfaction with the camp experience. All of these variables can be included as long as you ensure that the evaluation is quick to complete, easy to read (use terminology that parents and guardians, staff, and campers are familiar with; they are not camp professionals), and easy to submit.

Providing multiple responses as well as a comment section for each question is a good way to get the feedback you want. If you are interested in an overall picture of parents' and guardians' perceptions, multiple choice questions can provide descriptive statistics (mean, median, mode). Mean, median, and mode are numerical indicators that describe a situation rather than explain it (Muijs,

To get the most feedback from parents and guardians, your evaluation tool should be quick and easy. Focus on areas such as child safety, child fun, the daily schedule, discipline policies, communication policies, and the level of care provided by staff.

2004). They provide data that are relatively easy to interpret and apply because they don't require any inference on your part. For example, let's say you just want to know how many parents and guardians were satisfied with their overall camp experience. This question would appear on the survey, and the person analyzing the data would see that 80 percent of the respondents indicated that they were satisfied. This percentage describes the overall satisfaction rate, but it does not tell you why these respondents were satisfied nor does it say anything about the 20 percent who were not. You may decide not to change anything at this point because an 80 percent satisfaction rate exceeds your goal.

You may decide to look a little more closely at the data by extracting descriptive statistics for certain questions that address overall satisfaction with programs, staff, and the registration process. The statistics may indicate that parents and guardians were pleased with the registration process and staff but not with the programs. As a result, you decide to increase overall satisfaction from 80 to 90 percent for the next summer season by changing the programming. Deciding which programs to change and why moves your data analysis away from descriptive statistics and into inferential analysis or quantitative methods of evaluation. You determine which programming areas you need to improve based on qualitative feedback.

Multiple-choice questions allow you to assign number values to the answers, so you can use analytical software such as SPSS. Analytical software allows you to isolate answers to various questions and run statistics to better understand the responses. This form of analysis, called inferential analysis, goes beyond merely describing a situation. It has several options for isolating camp variables. We will consider causal-comparative relationships between answers or variables because those tend to be the most meaningful and easy to understand and apply in an organized camp setting.

Staying with the preceding example, let's say you want to learn how the respondents who indicated they were not satisfied with the camp experience answered the question about programming. In comparing these respondents' answers to the two questions, you notice, descriptively first, that those who were not happy with the programming were also not satisfied with the overall camp experience. Now, using analytical software that has formulas for inferential statistics, you run an analysis on the two questions to see whether a relationship exists between the two (the type of inferential statistics you run depends on your level of comfort with statistics and the type of software you are using). If you discover a relationship, you can reasonably assume that the cause of dissatisfaction with the overall camp experience was dissatisfaction with the programming. Although you cannot prove that this is true (and there is always the possibility that other factors affect this as well), it is a reasonable assumption on which to base a decision to make changes to the camp programming.

Be sure to include a large comment area for parents and guardians to write in so that you can learn some of the reasons they feel the way they do. However, keep in mind that these comments will not provide in-depth answers in the same way qualitative analysis does, which is discussed later in this chapter, but those comments are still valuable data. Finally, and perhaps most important, completing the survey should take no more than 12 minutes; this will ensure maximum participation (Muijs, 2004; Patton, 2002).

Camper Feedback

Surveys of campers are the most difficult to implement and extract meaningful data from because adults tend to downplay the camper's role in the success of a camp season. Indeed campers behave better if they are engaged, have fun, and must adhere to the rules of the camp to maintain the privilege of attending, which makes the camper feel good about their camp experience and makes the camp successful in reaching its goals. Campers who don't care about attending often do not care about rules, good sporting behavior, or punishment, which can undermine the success of the camp and the achievement of its goals.

Requesting authentic feedback from campers gives them a sense of ownership of their camp experience. More important, perhaps, is the fact that camper feedback, free of staff, peer, or parental influence, helps you understand the types of programs campers want. This information is more important than any feedback from staff and parents regarding procedures, protocols, and processes. You can solicit campers' advice, suggestions, and programming ideas by using kid-friendly surveys. (See CD-ROM form 8.3: Example of a Kid-Friendly Survey Form.)

FORM 8.3

Example of a Kid-Friendly Survey Form

1. What was your favorite thing about camp? _____

2. What was your least favorite thing about camp? _____

3. What other activities would you like to see at camp? _____

4. If you could change one thing about camp, what would it be? _____

Providing a kid-friendly survey is easier than you may imagine. However, there are some considerations to keep in mind. First, a kid-friendly survey should take no more than one minute to complete. Second, it should be taken one-on-one with a trained staff member who has been directed to ask questions and record the responses—without prompting. Third, a kid-friendly survey should be administered spontaneously during the camp day to avoid any parental influence. Fourth, you should not believe you have to survey every single camper; you need only a good representation of the camper population. This advice regarding kid-friendly surveys is based solely on my success in implementing this evaluative tool at camps across the United States.

Brevity is the most important characteristic of a kid-friendly survey. A one-minute survey asks an essential question that is directly related to the camper's experience. Typically this question is as simple as *What would you like to see the camp do more or less of?* or *What is something you want to learn to do or participate in at camp?* Another type of question addresses the outcomes or objectives of the camp. For example, if an identified outcome of the camp experience is to develop or introduce locomotive skills, an appropriate question might be *Show me how you skip, run, jump, strike* (and so on).

Because children (depending on their age) often respond very briefly, you may be able to ask more than one question during a one-minute survey. Children answering very short surveys often don't even realize that they are completing surveys. However, for older children, one minute may not be enough. If they speak longer than one minute, they should not be interrupted or cut off.

To decrease the possibility of peer influence, campers should be surveyed individually by a counselor whom they know. Having a private, positive (i.e., unrelated to behavior) moment with a counselor is important to children. Campers

Camper feedback can relate to the camper's experience (e.g., *What activities were your favorites?*) or to the camp's objectives (e.g., *Show me how you catch the ball.*).

see staff members taking time to ask about their experience, which confirms their confidence in the care and concern of the staff. Such meetings also give campers the opportunity to speak openly and honestly about their experience and what they want to do, wish they could do, or think the camp should do.

To decrease any influence the counselors conducting the survey may have on campers' answers, they must be very clear that their role is simply to ask the question and record the response. They must not prompt answers from children. This minimal training can easily be accommodated in a staff weekly meeting before initiating the kid-friendly surveys. Additionally, the questions should not be about staff, which would create discomfort and discourage children from speaking freely.

The responses that emerge from campers during kid-friendly surveys are important in several ways. First, these responses can inspire long-term program ideas and new initiatives that lead to camp improvement and evolution. Second, desires that are expressed by campers of various ages and experiences help you stay abreast of the desires and emerging needs of the community specific to child program development and camp trends. This information is extremely important for planning new programs or revitalizing existing ones. Third, depending on the question asked, camper perspectives can help you identify gaps in your goals, objectives, mission, and outcomes.

More often than not, kid-friendly surveys uncover staffing issues that were missed throughout the summer. Although most of these issues are minor, they are clearly major enough for campers to mention. Feedback about counselor care can point to portions of the staff training that you need to revise.

Let's say, in analyzing camper feedback, you discover that one group of counselors did not provide the same level of attention and care to campers who were minorities. The perceptions of these campers of this group of counselors indicate that more training around diversity, justice, and cultural competency needs to be incorporated into the staff training. However, if minority campers in other groups did not have similar perceptions of their counselors, you may determine that the training was effective because no other problems exist. You may further determine that the counselors in question have personal biases toward minorities, and you may decide not to invite them back.

Distribution of Evaluations

Chapter 2 discusses several methods of survey distribution for community needs. You can use the same methods for distributing camp evaluations as the summer season concludes. Focus groups, as previously discussed, do not require distribution; they simply require coordination and commitment. Most likely you will use the same process for distributing evaluations that you used to distribute your community needs assessment. The two most common types of evaluation distribution are in person and electronic.

If you decide to have a table at which parents and guardians can complete surveys at camper pickup, have it available every week so that you can get feedback from parents and guardians whose children attend for only one week. Incentives such as a discount for registration next year, a raffle, or camp paraphernalia may entice busy parents and guardians to stop and complete the survey, thereby maximizing participation.

Surveys may also be done via e-mail given that you likely have the e-mail addresses of all participants. E-mail surveys are better than in-person surveys because parents and guardians are more likely to complete them privately away from staff. However, the drawback to e-mail surveys is that there is no way to

CAMP STORIES

Developing an Evaluation Plan

The first summer I decided to implement a comprehensive evaluation plan, I was working at a camp in the Midwest, and my idea of *comprehensive* was getting the parents to complete a one-page form at the end of the summer. While this may not have been the best plan, I had to start somewhere, and so my strategy was to ask parents what they thought. In my zeal to examine the parental needs of the camp and in my rush to develop a survey, I forgot to ask some really important questions about counselor care, registration processes, and discipline policies. I recall distributing the survey in person to parents and thinking how progressive I was in soliciting their feedback so openly, when one parent came to me and said, "I don't understand how this is valuable. Why would I complete this?"

"What do you mean?" I asked.

"Well," she said, "I didn't attend this camp, so I have no idea if the program schedule was flexible, fun, and engaging. I do know that my kid loves to swim and that registering for this camp was difficult, but you have no questions about the things I can speak to, so I guess I will get my kid to fill this out."

I stared after her as she walked away because of course she was right; the evaluation tool I was using was nowhere near comprehensive enough, nor was it relevant to the group I was wishing to get feedback from. I felt sheepish, of course, but couldn't do much about it in terms of changing. After all, I had been using that tool all summer long, and we were in the final week of camp when the flawed instrument was brought to my attention. So I decided to keep using it and fix it next year. Despite my embarrassment and inexperience in assessing camp programs at the time, I decided that the data extracted from those surveys were still meaningful in that if parents had consulted their children about the program schedule, then at least I would get good feedback about that to make changes for the next summer. I realized, too, that if I wanted a truly comprehensive evaluation plan, then I would need to educate myself and ask for help from individuals who had more experience than me. I did both of those things and more, so in three years I had a truly comprehensive evaluation plan that I tweaked and refined each summer. The point is that I had to start somewhere and I didn't give up, despite my lack of knowledge and experience that first round. Honoring the process and committing to understanding how to improve the camp are imperative for camp administrators working to fulfill the mission of the program. When it comes to evaluation, it's not about perfection; it's about progress, and I encourage all practitioners to jump in—even if you are unsure how to swim!

shield parents' and guardians' identities. Those who are concerned about retribution toward their children for negative comments may not return e-mail surveys, decreasing your chance of obtaining maximum participation.

E-mail surveys are also easier than written surveys to manage in terms of data sorting and analysis. Online tools allow you to send reminders and resend e-mail links to parents and guardians who have not submitted the survey, because the danger of e-mails is that many people simply ignore them. When sending out a second, reminder e-mail, offer to send a hard copy of the evaluation via regular mail, or invite parents and guardians to fill out a survey in person when they come to pick up their camper (or both).

Because e-mail surveys arrive privately, parents and guardians can make up their minds about completing them without pressure from a staff member looking over their shoulders. Finally, e-mail surveys often result in more thoughtful and constructive responses than surveys completed by hand when adults are rushed to drop kids off or get kids home.

Another option is to use online distribution and submission of camp evaluations. Simply develop the evaluation tool using one of the several software tools, and e-mail the link to parents and guardians. A number of effective and free online survey programs, as discussed in chapter 2, are available. Maximum participation results in more meaningful quantitative data to be used for decision making during the analysis phase of the evaluation plan.

Evaluating Staff

You should evaluate every staff member and counselor-in-training (CIT) who may influence a camper's experience. Finding time to incorporate these evaluations into a busy camp week can be tricky, but planning, scheduling, and sharing the evaluation process with other members of the administrative staff can help you achieve this goal (see CD-ROM form 8.4: Suggested Timeline for Staff Evaluations). Offer opportunities for staff to reflect on their experience and their performance and to discuss those self-reflections in person with administrators. Consider incorporating the following evaluation tools for rating staff performance:

- Counselor self-evaluations
- Counselor-in-training self-evaluations (see CD-ROM form 8.5: CIT Evaluation)
- Administrative staff evaluations (see CD-ROM form 8.6: Director and Assistant Director Evaluations)
- Counselor-at-a-glance evaluations (see CD-ROM form 8.7: Log for Counselor-at-a-Glance and Midway Evaluations)
- Counselor final camp evaluations (see CD-ROM form 6.11: Counselor Final Camp Evaluation)

Formal and informal staff evaluations should take place during camp so that staff members can get feedback and take action to improve their performances. This constitutes half of your staff evaluation task; the other half is very simple.

Once you have received parent and guardian evaluations, you should compile your staff evaluation data to ascertain whether there are gaps between your perspective and parents' and guardians' perspectives of staff care. This important

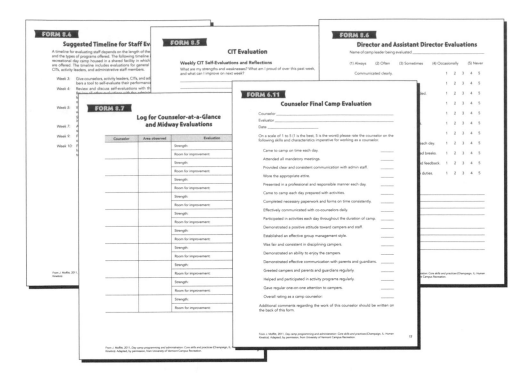

step is often overlooked. Take the time to compile, by staff member, parents' and guardians' thoughts about their work. This gives them another perspective that can help them grow even more. Those who may have believed that administrators were picking on them unfairly may see that others view their work similarly. Those who have received glowing reviews from the administration may receive additional suggestions and areas of improvement from parent evaluations that would have otherwise been overlooked.

If you lack the time or the online tools to make such a compilation, simply review the descriptive statistics provided by the staff evaluations and parent evaluations and draw conclusions. For example, if both you and parents rank camper care low, you have some work to do in developing your staff. On the other hand, if you rank your counselors high but parents and guardians rank them low, this may imply that you need to hire more staff.

You can use staff evaluations when deciding which counselors to invite back and who will receive positive references should they decide to move on from the organization. For example, you may decide to invite back only the counselors who achieve a certain level of competency. A solid evaluation process will allow you to justify your decisions to organizational leaders or the human resources department, if necessary.

Journal Entries

Journal entries can be very helpful for giving you a comprehensive picture of your camp. Take time daily or weekly to write down your thoughts, suggestions,

CAMP COUNSEL

Journaling at Camp

Journaling at camp is a worthwhile endeavor because camp is busy and you may not be able to remember everything you want to do, change, or discard if you do not take the time to write down notes. Your notes can be about anything: processes, programs, feelings, or things to keep in mind for the summer to follow. However, finding the time to journal and doing so in a meaningful way can be difficult. Follow the tips below to help you manage these difficulties so that journaling can become a staple of your evaluation plan for years to come.

- Schedule journaling time as part of your duties.
- Be reflective in your journal entries. Do not write just for the sake of writing; try to capture the needs of the camp—which are being met, which are not, and how can the camp change and evolve?
- Do not try to journal every day. Weekly is fine.
- Carry your journal around camp. That way, journaling can happen organically as you notice things so that you don't have to write from memory.
- Ask other camp leaders or staff members to journal to provide more breadth and depth to the evaluation process.

concerns, successes, and failures; these may turn out to be more meaningful for decision making than statistical data. You can use your journal entries as a blueprint for the evaluation process.

Journal entries provide qualitative data that can be analyzed in tandem with other documents and data during triangulation analysis (see chapter 2). Additionally, your journal can document the progress of the camp over time and identify changes that were made to address an issue, which may have failed. In the future, when similar ideas are generated for the same issue, the journal can help you refine the solution until you succeed.

Finding time in a busy camp day or week to sit down and write in a journal can be difficult. Do not get too tied up with finding a consistent time to write. Instead, develop a note-taking system and jot notes in your journal at random times throughout the day. Finding what works for you is an important step in creating this habitual practice.

Data Analysis

Regardless of the method of data collection you have chosen, you have to analyze the results in a way that makes sense to you so that you can make changes that allow the camp to evolve. Generally speaking, the concerns of parents and guardians, campers, and staff should be the baseline for determining the overall satisfaction with and success of the camp before determining specific issues that need attention. The camp should be in a very good position to do just this if you have surveyed all three stakeholders and gathered the data. Now you must interpret that data.

Although you can interpret data in any one of a number of ways, many argue that the easiest and most practical interpretations can be achieved through descriptive statistics as discussed earlier in this chapter. In addition, extracting themes from focus groups is time-consuming but relatively easy, very meaningful, and likely to be immediately applicable to the camp in terms of making changes.

Data interpretation as outlined in this section includes a review of the responses of all stakeholders. Admittedly, this is time-consuming and requires experience and practice, but it offers the hope of finding something that you have missed or something that is creating stagnation in your programming. Because most camp programs are concerned with overall satisfaction rates, the process described here has the goal of satisfaction in mind.

Begin your analysis with the parent and guardian evaluation forms. Use descriptive statistics to paint a general picture of whether patrons believe the camp satisfied their expectations. Statistically identify the areas patrons believe the camp struggled with the most and the areas in which the camp was the most successful. These are areas that affect overall satisfaction. As a quantitative evaluation, you can select certain questions and review the statistics on those questions to see more detail about what the stakeholders believe made the camp a more or less satisfying experience. Again, you can use descriptive statistics for each question or begin to look at relationships between questions using SPSS tools, if they are available and you are comfortable with the software. During this process, the top issues that affected overall satisfaction begin to emerge.

Next, review data from staff evaluations, staff meetings, and the staff focus group. The point here is to determine whether the biggest issues identified by parents and guardians were also identified by the staff throughout the course of the program. If the answer to this question is yes, then you know that two of the three stakeholders view the problem similarly. Therefore, the issue is worthy of review. Now, review the journal entries that were completed by administrators to understand why (and if) this issue was overlooked by the camp leaders. This is an important part of the process because it identifies whether the issue was missed because of a lack of resources, poor judgment, or a lack of awareness.

You may want to read the testimonials of campers to further ascertain whether they noticed the issue. If so, then the issue is affecting every stakeholder and should be a top priority for troubleshooting. Camper feedback is important for programming, but it should be used in conjunction with staff and parent and guardian feedback when making decisions about such things as registration processes, camp policies, and operational procedures. These are relevant to the camp but have minimal impact on campers' experiences.

This process of data analysis can be used for any goal you may identify. This is the simplest form of triangulating data. Although it may not be the most rigorous, it is the most relevant and practical for camp programs. In other words, the process provides an enormous return on your initial investments in the form of meaningful results that are representative of the unique nature of your programs from planning to evaluation. These results point to the issues you should address in future summer seasons.

Camp programs lend themselves to multiple perspectives on their success. Ignoring one stakeholder over another will not build your camp's reputation and result in reaching your goals. Although there are many instances in which you will have to make a decision in favor of one stakeholder or another, do not ignore the needs and issues that are relevant to all stakeholders.

Conclusion

Evaluation processes that reveal the thoughts, ideas, concerns, needs, and suggestions of staff, parents and guardians, and campers are very valuable. Staff focus groups provide good supplemental qualitative data for the staff evaluation process that was discussed in chapter 6 and highlighted again in this chapter.

Online distribution of camp evaluations to parents and guardians is highly recommended. An important evaluation that is often overlooked is that of your primary service population—campers. Kid-friendly surveys can help you determine their needs.

Formal staff evaluations obtained during camp can be used during the evaluation period to garner more in-depth information about issues you may need to address. You should also develop the habit of recording observations in journal entries, which can be enormously helpful during data analysis. You will then need to interpret the collected data to inform future decision making.

New camp programs can use the basic tools and considerations in this chapter to develop a solid evaluation process. Existing camp programs can revise their evaluation plans and incorporate some of the suggestions to determine the top concerns of their stakeholders. Implementing a solid evaluation process is an important step in building the camp's reputation and laying a foundation for continued success.

REFERENCES

American Camp Association (ACA). (2010a). *About ACA*. Retrieved from www.acacamps. org/about/celebrating-150-years-camp-moments

American Camp Association (ACA). (2010b). *Camp trends fact sheet*. Retrieved from www. acacamps.org/media-center/camp-trends/fact

American Camp Association (ACA). (2010c). *Media center: Benefits of camp*. Retrieved from www.acacamps.org/media-center/benefits-of-camp

Ball, A., & Ball, B. (1995). *Basic camp management: An introduction to camp administration* (4th ed.). Martinsville, IN: American Camp Association.

Canadian Parks and Recreation Association. (1998). *Impact and benefits of physical activity and recreation on Canadian youth-at-risk*. Retrieved from www.lin.ca

Centers for Disease Control and Prevention (CDC). (2008). *Food-safe schools action guide*. Retrieved from www.cdc.gov/healthyyouth/foodsafety/actionguide.htm

Cronin, J. (2009). Upgrading to Web 2.0: An experiential project to build a marketing Wiki. *Journal of Marketing Education, 31* (1), 66-75 (ERIC Document Reproduction Service No. EJ831770).

Dennis, M. (2006). *A practical guide to enrollment and retention management in higher education*. Westport, CT: Bergin & Garvey.

Diana, A. (2001). *Youth at play: Preventing youth problem behavior through sport and recreation*. Unpublished master's thesis, University of Oregon, Eugene.

Ditter, B. (1995). New directions in staff training and development. *Camping Magazine, 67* (3), 38-42 (ERIC Document Reproduction Service No. EJ505585).

Ditter, B. (2001). A key set of skills for counselors: In the trenches. *Camping Magazine, 74* (3), 12-14 (ERIC Document Reproduction Service No. EJ627027).

Dottavio, F., O'Leary, J., & Koth, B. (1980). The social group variable in recreation participation studies. *Journal of Leisure Research, 12*, 357-367.

Draper, B.J. (1975). *The effect of camping on self concept*. Unpublished master's thesis, University of Kentucky, Lexington.

Duncan, M. (1956). *The interest and needs of older girls as influencing factors in the development of camp programs*. Unpublished master's thesis, University of North Carolina, Greensboro.

Edwards, P. (2000). Evidence-based strategies for increasing participation in physical activity in community recreation, fitness and sport. *Active Ontario*. Retrieved from www.lin.ca

Fletcher, S.A. (1973). *A comparison of affective changes between economically disadvantaged sixth graders at a resident outdoor education program*. Unpublished doctoral dissertation, Indiana University, Bloomington.

Freeburg, W. (1949). *Law and liability of municipal, charitable and private corporations for conducting recreation camps*. Unpublished doctoral dissertation, Indiana University, Bloomington.

Grimmer, K., & Williams, J. (2001). Young people's participation in sports and recreational activities and associated injuries. *ACHPER-Australia, 8* (2-3), 3-4 (Sport Discus Document Reproduction Service No. S-793575).

Harter, S. (1990). Issues in the assessment of the self concept of children and adolescents. In A. LaGreca (Ed.), *Through the eyes of the child: Obtaining self-reports from children and adolescents* (pp. 292-325). Boston: Allyn & Bacon.

Hartmann, D. (2001). Notes on midnight basketball and the cultural politics of recreation, race, and at-risk urban youth. *Journal of Sport and Social Issues, 25,* 339-271. Abstract retrieved from Sport Discus Database (Sport Discus Document Reproduction Service No. S-796232).

Henderson, K. (1996). Just recreation for girls and women. *Journal of Physical Education, Recreation and Dance, 67* (2), 45-46. Retrieved from *Periodical Abstract Research II Edition* with full text database No. 02515941.

Henderson, K., Bialeschki, M., Hemmingway, J., Hodges, J., Kivel, B., & Sessoms, D. (2001). *Introduction to recreation and leisure.* State College, PA: Venture.

Hulett, F. (1960). *A quantitative and qualitative study of facilities for school camping and outdoor education on state owned lands in Illinois.* Unpublished doctoral dissertation, University of Oregon, Eugene.

Hultsmann, W. (1999). Promoting physical activity through parks and recreation: A focus on youth and adolescence. *Journal of Physical Education, Recreation, and Dance, 70* (2), 66-67. Retrieved from *Periodical Abstract Research II Edition* with full text database No. 03786447.

Jensen, C. (1977). *Leisure and recreation: Introduction and overview.* Philadelphia: Lea & Febiger.

Lantz, E. (1955). *A prospectus for the administration of college and university camps.* Unpublished master's thesis, University of California, Los Angeles.

Lee, R.G. (1972). The social definition of outdoor recreation places. In W.R. Burch, N. Cheek, & L. Taylor (Eds.), *Social behavior, natural resources, and environment* (pp. 68-84). New York: Harper & Row.

Lefstein, L., Kerewsky, W., Medrich, E., & Frank, C. (1982). *3:00 to 6:00 p.m.: Young adolescents at home and in the community.* Center for Early Adolescence, University of North Carolina Chapel Hill (ERIC Document Reproduction Service No. ED222247).

Likert, R. (1932). A technique for the measurement of attitudes. *Archives of Psychology, 22* (140), 1-55.

Marsh, P. (1999). *What does camp do for kids? A meta-analysis of the influence of organized camping experience on the self-constructs of youth.* Unpublished thesis, University of Oregon, Eugene.

Maurer-Starks, S. (2003). Preparing your staff for emergencies. *Camping Magazine, 76* (2), 41-43 (ERIC Document Reproduction Service No. EJ668557).

McConnell, S. (1996). Is your waterfront safe? Creating an emergency action plan. *Camping Magazine, 68* (5), 43-44 (ERIC Document Reproduction Service No. EJ528291).

Mourão-Carvalhal, I., Vasconcelos-Raposo, J., & Malina, R. (2001). How boys and girls spend their free time. *Exercise and Society Journal of Sport Science, 28,* 114. Abstract retrieved from the Sport Discus Database (Sport Discus Document Reproduction Service No. S-793940).

Muijs, D. (2004). *Doing quantitative research in education with SPSS.* Thousand Oaks, CA: Sage.

Northern Arizona University. (2001). *Organized camping: What is it?* Retrieved from www.prm.nau.edu/prm280/chap1_lesson.htm

Ontario (Canada) Ministry of Citizenship, Culture and Recreation; SMC Management Services, Inc.; and Grassroots Enterprises. (1998). *Developing a recreation framework for children and youth.* Retrieved from www.lin.ca

Pate, R., Heath, G., Dowda, M., & Trost, S. (1996). Associations between physical activity and other health behaviors in a representative sample of U.S. adolescents. *American Journal of Public Health, 86,* 1577-1581.

Patton, M. (2002). *Qualitative research and evaluation methods.* Thousand Oaks, CA: Sage.

Pawelko, K., & Magafus, A. (1997). Leisure well-being among adolescent groups: Time choices and self-determination (Report No. 0031-2215). *Journal of Parks and Recreation, 32* (7), 28-39 (Eric Document Reproduction Service No. EJ550008).

Pellegrini, A. (1992). Preference for outdoor play during early adolescence. *Journal of Adolescence, 15,* 241-254. Retrieved from *Periodical Abstracts Research II Edition* with full text database No. 01083373.

Pershing, J.A. (2000). *USCG workshop survey: The design and development of survey instruments.* Bloomington, IN: Education and Management Research Associates.

Phillip, S. (1998). Race and gender differences in adolescent peer group approval of leisure activities. *Journal of Leisure Research, 30,* 214-232. Retrieved from *Periodical Abstract Research II Edition* with full text database No. 03453676.

Ramsing, R. (2007). Organized camping: A historical perspective. *Journal of Child and Adolescent Psychiatric Clinics of North America, 16* (4), 751-754.

Ravenscroft, N., & Markwell, S. (2000). Ethnicity and the integration and exclusion of young people through urban park and recreation provision. *Managing Leisure, 5* (3), 135-150. Abstract retrieved from Sport Discus Database (Sport Discus Document Reproduction Service No. S-797115).

Rothschild, J. (2001). Adding character to camp programs: Using ropes courses to teach values. *Camping Magazine, 74* (4), 19-21. Abstract retrieved from Sport Discus Database (Sport Discus Document Reproduction Service No. S-783878).

Ruiz, A. (2000). Tracking physical activity from childhood to adolescence. *Journal of Physical Education, Recreation, and Dance, 71* (30), 10. Retrieved from *Periodical Abstract Research II Edition* with full text database No. 50871032.

Rule, M. (1998). *Resident camp directors and wilderness: Attitudes, characteristics, and opinions.* Unpublished master's thesis, Washington State University, Pullman.

Shivers, J. (1989). *Camping: Organization and operation.* Englewood Cliffs, NJ: Prentice Hall.

Sibthorp, R. (2000). *Instrument validation and multivariate assessment of life skill development in adolescents through the adventure education process.* Unpublished doctoral dissertation, Indiana University, Bloomington.

Smith, C. (1991, September). *Overview of youth recreation programs in the United States.* Washington, DC: Carnegie Council on Adolescent Development (ERIC Document Reproduction Service No. ED360268).

Sullivan, K., & O'Brien, M. (2001). Inclusive programming at summer camp. *Parks and Recreation, 36* (5), 66-72.

Taylor, C. (2001). Generation yes: How does a leisure provider find out what young people want from their services and can young people be engaged in the decision-making process? *Leisure Manager, 19* (5), 23-24. Abstract retrieved from the Sport Discus Database (Sport Discus Document Reproduction Service No. S-765633).

Taylor, W., Blair, S., Cummings, S., Wun, C., & Malina, R. (1999). Childhood and adolescent physical activity patterns and adult physical activity. *American College of Sports Medicine, 31,* 118-123.

Thurber, C.A., Scanlin, M.M., Scheuler, L., & Henderson, K.A. (2007). Youth development outcomes of the camp experience: Evidence for multidimensional growth. *Journal of Youth Adolescence, 36,* 241-254.

Trudeau, F., Laurencelle, L., Tremblay, J., Rice, M., & Shephard, R. (1999). Daily primary physical education: Effects on physical activity during adult life. *American College of Sports Medicine, 31,* 111-117.

Tuckman, B., & Jensen, M. (1977). Stages of small group development revisited. *Group and Organization Studies, 2* (4), 419-426 (ERIC Document Reproduction Service No. EJ175336).

Walton, M. (2001). Planning for play. *Leisure Manager, 19* (10), 24-25. Abstract retrieved from Sport Discus Database (Sport Discus Document Reproduction Service No. S-792432).

Warder, D. (1973). *Self-concepts and activity preference of participants of seven organized summer outdoor residential camps*. Unpublished master's thesis, University of Oregon, Eugene.

West, S., & Crompton, J. (2001). A review of the impact of adventure programming on at-risk youth. *Journal of Parks and Recreation Administration, 19,* 113-140. Abstract retrieved from Sport Discus Database (Sport Discus Document Reproduction Service No. S-787911).

Widmer, M., Ellis, G., & Trunnell, E. (1996). Measurement of ethical behavior in leisure among high and low risk adolescents. *Journal of Adolescence, 31,* 397-408. Retrieved from *Periodical Abstract Research II Edition* with full text database No. 02609631.

Willits, W., & Willits, F. (1986). Adolescent participation in leisure activities: The "less the more" or "the more the more"? *Leisure Studies, 8,* 189-206.

Note: Page numbers followed by an italicized *f* or *t* represent figures or tables found on those pages, respectively.

Jill Moffitt, EdD, is director of campus recreation and student life at the University of North Carolina at Asheville. She has administered day camp programs in colleges, nonprofit organizations, private clubs, and municipal settings and has operated sport camps and overnight camps as well. Since 1998, she has run camp operations and has been called on to present on day camps at state, regional, and national conferences.

She developed UNC Asheville's day camp program from scratch and has consulted with other colleges in assessing student learning outcomes in higher education student affairs or student services departments. An AmeriCorps veteran, Moffitt is a member of the National Intramural-Recreational Sports Association, NASPA Student Affairs Administrators in Higher Education, and Athletic Business. She earned her EdD in educational leadership and policy studies from the University of Vermont and received an Outstanding University Collaborator Award from UNC Asheville in 2009 and an Outstanding Program Award from AmeriCorps in 2000.

You'll find other outstanding
recreation resources at
www.HumanKinetics.com

In the U.S. call 1.800.747.4457
Australia 08 8372 0999
Canada. 1.800.465.7301
Europe . . . . .+44 (0) 113 255 5665
New Zealand 0800 222 062

HOW TO USE THE CD-ROM

System Requirements

You can use this CD-ROM on either a Windows-based PC or a Macintosh computer.

Windows

- IBM PC compatible with Pentium processor
- Windows 2000/XP/Vista/7
- Adobe Reader 8.0
- 4x CD-ROM drive

Macintosh

- Power Mac recommended
- System 10.4 or higher
- Adobe Reader
- 4x CD-ROM drive

User Instructions

Windows

1. Insert the *Day Camp Programming and Administration* CD-ROM. (Note: The CD-ROM must be present in the drive at all times.)
2. Select the "My Computer" icon from the desktop.
3. Select the CD-ROM drive.
4. Open the file you wish to view. See the "00Start.pdf" file for a list of the contents.

Macintosh

1. Insert the *Day Camp Programming and Administration* CD-ROM. (Note: The CD-ROM must be present in the drive at all times.)
2. Double-click the CD icon located on the desktop.
3. Open the file you wish to view. See the "00Start" file for a list of the contents.

For customer support, contact Technical Support:

Phone: 217-351-5076 Monday through Friday (excluding holidays) between 7:00 a.m. and 7:00 p.m. (CST).

Fax: 217-351-2674

E-mail: support@hkusa.com